P. Allen Smith's
Bringing the Garden
INDOORS

P. Allen Smith's
Bringing the Garden
INDOORS

Containers, Crafts, and Bouquets for Every Room

PHOTOGRAPHS BY JANE COLCLASURE AND KELLY QUINN
DESIGN BY DINA DELL'ARCIPRETE/DK DESIGN PARTNERS, INC.

CLARKSON POTTER/PUBLISHERS
NEW YORK

Library of Congress Cataloging-in-Publication Data
    P. Allen Smith's bringing the garden indoors / P. Allen Smith; photographs by Jane Colclasure and
Kelly Quinn. — 1st ed. Includes index.
1. Indoor gardening. I. Title. II. Title: Bringing the garden indoors
SB419.S555 2009
747'.98—dc22   2008014868

ISBN 978-0-307-35109-8

Printed in China

10 9 8 7 6 5 4 3 2 1

First Edition

To D. Garner, Jr., C. Miller, Jr., and W. A. Lile
for sharing their inspired sense of design

Weaving the beauty of the natural world into the style of a home is something that has intrigued me throughout my life and career. It's a central theme found at the heart of the garden home. My enthusiasm for this activity was nurtured during my childhood, when much of my time was spent outdoors. From dawn to dusk, the boundaries of my world were defined not by four walls and a roof but by places that I could roam on foot, bicycle, or a horse. Each morning I found it hard to contain my desire to bolt out the door and begin a new adventure in the fields and forests that surrounded my home. That's where I found that life held its most exciting possibilities.

My view of the world and how it works was shaped by doing farm chores, running through crop fields, catching tadpoles, swimming in streams, growing gardens, raising chickens, and playing in the barn. Only nightfall or hunger could drive me inside with my pockets stuffed full of found treasures. Anything that caught my attention and warranted closer study was displayed in my room: rocks, plants, old bottles, pieces of wood, and an assortment of snakes, bugs, and other fascinating animals. Soon my bedroom took on the look of the out-of-doors and I began thinking of both realms, indoors and out, as my home.

This growing habit of dragging things inside drove my mother to distraction, as it was hard to keep up with a house full of terrariums, aquariums, and incubators along with four active children. But thankfully, she put up with my ever-growing collections, even as they spilled into other parts of the house.

It was during those formative years that my interest in natural forms grew. I found comfort in the beauty of their designs and was enthralled with their colors, textures, and shapes. I still enjoy marveling at the simplest things just as I did as a child. And I continue to litter my mantels, shelves, and table surfaces with objects found along the way, whether they are discovered on a walk through the woods, along a beach, or in a junk shop. I have come to believe that being surrounded by nature is one of the best ways to learn good design sense.

As I reflect on my career as a garden designer, I find its development has echoes of my youthful past. As I began my work with clients, I enjoyed creating gardens with colorful flower borders that were displayed in well-landscaped spaces. But soon my interest evolved into designs for areas closer to the house such as patios, terraces, and decks, and I enjoyed mixing plants with tables and chairs to define the function of these settings as places for dining, relaxing, and entertaining. As the choices in more stylish outdoor furnishings grew, so did my ideas in treating these areas to look more like interior rooms. Soon I was encouraging my clients to imagine pushing the walls of their homes outside to create a series of uniquely personal garden rooms. By merging the look and feel of interior and exterior areas, homeowners began to consider both places as rooms in their home, just as I did as a child. The division between inside and out softened as the look of both areas belonging together developed.

In my earlier Garden Home books, I explored ways to create garden rooms outside. Now it only seems natural to take the next step and invite you inside my home so you can see how a home's interior can be enlivened when touched by nature's hand. My desire to share this idea comes at a time when I feel the need more than ever for us all to be closely connected to our natural surroundings. Bringing the outdoors *in* provides a reassuring link to the broader idea of the garden that nurtures us all. My hope is that as you bring more of the garden inside, you, too, will feel an increased sense of well-being.

As I open the doors to my home, you'll see that I am a hopeless collector. That's a part of my youth I never outgrew. The gardener side of my personality enjoys creating arrangements with flowers, foliage, dried plants, seedpods, branches, vegetables, and fruits, while my "object finder" side likes the challenge of mixing garden gleanings with pieces from my collections to add art and visual interest to the display. It's the sort of thing one can do on any budget. You can ramp it up to the most sought after pieces of eighteenth-century porcelain or find an equal amount of satisfaction in acquiring a set of low-cost transferware dishes popular during the Depression. There is something exhilarating in the juxtaposition among the found, the collected, and the natural. Since we all tend to collect something, I hope you find my mix to be a creative springboard for your own creations. I've also added examples of arrangements in other homes to demonstrate how these ideas can be adapted in rooms with any decor.

Opposite, clockwise from top left: An eclectic collection of treasures, including quartz crystals, a Paris porcelain vase filled with white feathers, seashells from the beach, and an alabaster bust of Columbus, adorn the fireplace mantel in my foyer. An outdoor chandelier suspended from an overhanging tree branch turns this fresh-air setting into an elegant dining room. Sweet hellebores, one of the first flowers to bloom each year, make a welcome display planted in one of my brown transferware soup tureens. The rich bronze color of wild and Bosc pears adds a golden accent next to the fall pear cake.

This book has four chapters that illustrate living areas that are common to every home: entrances, the kitchen and dining area, living room or family room, bedroom and bath; and I couldn't resist adding one more room—an outdoor dining spot, because I firmly believe that no home should be without some place, even if it's seating for one, where a meal can be enjoyed alfresco.

My 1904 Colonial Revival cottage is located in a historic district of Little Rock, and the antique furnishings in my home reflect the period style of the neighborhood as well as the exterior of the house. I started collecting antiques because I thought they were more interesting than the freshly minted tables, dressers, and chairs found in furniture stores. And truth be told, when I first moved into this house, I couldn't afford new furniture. I don't mind the chips and cracks, worn edges, and missing bits. To me that means if the objects could talk they would have an even better story to tell. And once I started collecting antiques, it became a fun and entertaining hobby.

Whether we want to admit it or not, we are all collectors—just look through any cupboard, closet, or garage in America, and there you'll find objects of desire that at one time or another someone gathered and stored away. I understand this compulsion. What some might call clutter, I view as a "richly appointed" interior with lots of interesting items, each with its own story.

Our homes and gardens are such personal expressions of ourselves. The way we interact within these two realms can bring greater balance and harmony to our lives and raise our consciousness about the natural world. If you are like me, throughout your life you have surrounded yourself with objects that have meaning to you. After time, they become somewhat invisible because we get so used to seeing them. Many of the objects in my collections have special significance and others are merely decorative or functional. My vision of creating a garden home is about bringing all these objects to life in new and stylish ways by merging them with the gardens just outside the doors of our homes. To help you envision these ideas, they are presented in various rooms of the house. The displays are meant to serve as a creative springboard for your own designs and can be used anywhere you want to add a special accent. I believe that bringing our gardens and collections together in beautiful expressions is one of the best ways to blur the lines between inside and out.

Opposite: One of the joys of having a garden is to bring plants indoors to enliven a home's interior. Each week I look for something new that has reached its prime, and I eagerly await the day when my drift of 'Lady Jane' tulips comes into flower. The petals are fragile, so I've found they last longer if I put just a few blooms in a glass vessel such as champagne flutes. To make the most of the flowers, I group several glasses together and then place them on a mirror to double their volume. Votive candlelight is the final touch that illuminates the display and adds sparkle to the arrangement.

Entrances

Because it's *your* home, every part of it becomes a reflection of you—your personality, interests, and outlook on life. One area that is often overlooked for its potential to connect the garden with the home is the entry. Outside, it is the place to "show a little leg" and reveal a bit of your home's interior style, so make it memorable. Look upon this space as an opportunity to extend visitors a warm welcome even before you greet them at the door. As the saying goes, you never get a second chance to make a first impression, and both front- and back-door entrances are places where that first impression of your home's interior are formed. Whether your entry is grand or humble, treat the area as equal to a room in your home and set the tone of your welcome with tantalizing hints of things to come.

As guests approach your door and wait to enter, they have time to pause and look around, taking in the surroundings. The elements you choose to accent the entry create its sense of style. It's not so much about the number of items you assemble as it is about where you place them. I often try to imagine myself as a first-time visitor to my home. As I leave my car and walk up the pathway to the front door, I notice what visitors see along the way. I've found that a few well-placed displays that mix plants with items from my favorite collections help to draw their attention, slow their pace, and have them looking forward to seeing what's inside.

And since there are two sides to every door, with different experiences on each side, I like to provide a sense of continuity with garden-themed accents as soon as they enter. Crossing a threshold is a magical point of transition that divides public spaces from personal zones. By combining interior furnishings with plants and other reminders of the garden, your foyer or entryway serves as a seamless transition.

If you thumb through books and magazines on interior design, you'll see how often a houseplant, garden urn, landscape print, flower arrangement, botanical print, or other garden-inspired accent is used to enliven the space. These elements bring an undeniable sense of beauty and well-being to every room, and the entry, by virtue of its location, is the first place in your home where you can add those important details to define your garden-home style.

Opposite, clockwise from top left: Simple does it in this winter entryway arrangement, where a rustic window box is filled with fresh pine boughs, mini pinecones serve as a topper at the base of the potted Frasier fir, and a moss-topped container and a pot filled with bright red heavenly bamboo berries (*Nandina domestica*) add eye-catching colors and textures. Varying the heights within this fall display makes the most of the ensemble; chrysanthemums, ivy, coleus, ornamental grass, and pumpkins combine to capture the essence of the season. A collection of colorfully planted summer containers softens the hard lines of the steps and the porch railing to create a more welcoming feel. Few things say spring more than a bouquet of tulips: to create this look, pack bulbs "shoulder to shoulder" in a large container in the fall and leave them in a cool protected area over winter.

1. Roll Out the Welcome Mat

Greet your guests even before they knock on your door with touches of the garden along the way. Punctuate the walk with an ensemble of planted pots or line the outer edges of your steps with clusters of containers filled with colorful flowers and foliage. It's a beautiful way to embellish the pathway and guide visitors along.

As a time-saving tip, rather than combining several different varieties of plants in a container, try filling each pot with a single variety. Then create beautiful arrangements by clustering several containers together and freshen the display by swapping pots in and out. If there is a lull in a plant's performance, simply replace it with one that's in its prime. Change the display to suit your mood, the time of year, or to brighten up a spot along the path that needs a little something extra. As you assemble the containers, don't be shy; think big and be generous by grouping several containers together for real impact.

cluster containers for bold effect

MAKE AN IMPRESSION As you plant each container, combine several small plants of the same variety or buy a large one so as soon as it's planted, it is full and ready for display. The effect is diminished when you have to wait several weeks for the plants to grow out.

SAVE YOUR BACK Large containers can be quite heavy once they are filled with soil and plants. Make it easy on yourself by planting them where they will be displayed.

NOTE THE GROWING CONDITIONS Choose plants that grow best in the light and wind conditions where the containers will be growing.

CHOOSE THE RIGHT CONTAINERS Vary the heights and sizes of the pots in a grouping for best effect. The roots of shrubs and perennials require more soil and deeper pots than annuals. Make sure all containers have drainage holes, and place saucers underneath them to protect surfaces.

Above: Varying the sizes of the containers gathered on this entry gives the plantings more impact. **Left:** Scale the size of your containers to the area. Smaller pots would be overlooked in this setting. **Opposite:** Long-blooming annuals such as petunias and geraniums along with lilies and the colorful foliage of coleus accent the steps to the front door.

2. *Change the Scenery*

As the seasons turn, transform the displays around your doorway to reflect the changing landscape. It's all part of being in tune with nature's rhythms and a way to enhance the gardenlike quality of your home. Depending on the amount of time you want to spend, you can style your doorway for special events and holidays or create long-lasting displays that have more of a seasonal flavor. Consider how rooms in your home feel different through the year. The passing of the seasons not only heralds a change in temperature but also affects quality of light, which in turn has an effect on the way we feel both physically and emotionally. Reflecting these changing moods in the decor around our doorways is both evocative and invigorating.

LIGHT THE WAY

Unpack those strings of winter holiday lights and weave them along the ground through flower beds bordering walkways to your home's entries. Lightly cover the cords with moss or mulch and create a softly illuminated path to your door.

Above left: The window box and containers reflect the abundance of the season; they are filled with a colorful assortment of flowering and foliage plants, including 'Infinity Dark Pink' New Guinea impatiens, 'Goldilocks' creeping Jenny, 'Fishnet Stockings' coleus, 'Charmed Wine' shamrock, 'Dolce Key Lime Pie' coral bells, 'Jelly Bean Rose' impatiens, and 'Evergold' sedge. **Above right:** A blend of salmon-pink and purple tulips announces that it's spring. **Opposite:** Much like the tablescapes that you display in your house, this exterior winter arrangement combines things that are on hand in the garden, such as pots, grapevine wreaths, and cuttings from plants.

seasonal ideas

SPRING Until the temperatures even out, use plants in your displays that can take the ups and downs of the weather, such as crocuses, primroses, daffodils, tulips, pansies, violas, lettuce, hyacinths, fresh rye grass, nemesia, and violets. These plants have their own "antifreeze" that can take nighttime temperatures in the mid-20s without blinking. Accessories such as decorated eggs, straw-filled baskets, and colorful umbrellas serve as symbols of the season.

SUMMER As the energy of spring throttles down and the heat of July and August takes over, it's time to create refreshing scenes that cool and beckon the visitor to pause at your doorway. Match the plants you use to your entry's light conditions. Full-sun plants include daisies, sedums, miniature roses, and coleus, while shade plants could be blousy ferns, impatiens, tropical plants, and begonias. Tabletop water gardens add a refreshing touch. Give houseplants a summer vacation and make them part of the display.

FALL As leaves spiral down to blanket the garden in a carpet of colors, thoughts of collecting and storing the harvest seem to be the order of the day. Plants that reflect the spirit of the season are ornamental grasses, chrysanthemums, rosemary, kale, asters, dahlias, sunflowers, and marigolds as well as pumpkins and gourds. Fall decorations are meant to reflect the rewards of the growing season, so make your displays generous and colorful. Pack containers with loads of vibrant flowers and pile gourds and pumpkins in window boxes accented with branches of bittersweet.

WINTER Keep your entry looking friendly and inviting by accenting your doorway and windows with seasonal plants and colorful accents. If you enjoy mild winters, you can continue to grow and display cool-season plants such as pansies, ornamental kale, heather, and violas outside your door. But if temperatures regularly dip below freezing, arrangements of evergreen boughs, berried limbs, pinecones, or branches that have interesting shapes or colorful bark anchored in weatherproof vessels add interest and style. Some containerized shrubs and small trees suited for your climate can also be overwintered around your door.

Top: A white-themed collection of spring flowers and herbs gives this entry a refreshing feel. **Above:** On a trip to San Diego, I brought home this whimsical purse topiary, planted in a variety of succulents and designed by Margee Rader, to give to a friend. She placed it by her entry and enjoyed all the comments from visiting friends. **Opposite:** Pumpkins hollowed out and filled with containers of ornamental grass—'Leatherleaf' sedge, 'Hameln' fountain grass, and 'Frosty Curls' sedge—and highlighted with strings of battery-powered LED lights make a playful autumn display.

PLANT COLLECTIONS

Fruits and Vegetables

I find growing vegetables to be just as satisfying and reward-ing as growing flowers, and I always make room in my garden for both. I'm sure this comes from my family's her-itage of having a large vegetable garden and my own enjoy-ment of eating fresh home-grown produce. But even as I was piling food on my plate, I found pleasure in the decorative effect of fruits and vegetables in the home. A simple bowl full of freshly polished apples in the middle of a table is always appealing. The colors, forms, and textures of fruits and vegetables are beautiful in their own right or in combination with other garden elements. Broadening the view of garden-inspired accents beyond flowers offers you more possibilities to decorate your home.

1. *Wild pears (Pyrus communis)*

2. *'Early Long Purple' eggplant (Solanum melongena)*

3. *Pumpkin mix (Cucurbita pepo, C. moschata, and C. maxima)*

4. *'Carnival' squash (Cucurbita pepo)*

5. *Tomato mix (Lycopersicon esculentum)*

6. *'One Too Many' squash (Cucurbita maxima)*

7. *Lemons/limes (Citrus limon and C. limetta)*

8. *'Mickylee' watermelon (Cirullus lanatus var. lanatus)*

9. *Kieffer pears (Pyrus hybrid)*

3. Frame the View

Adorning an area to draw attention to an object or view is a time-honored principle of garden design, so why not use it to your advantage at your home's entrance? Accenting windows with colorful displays both inside and out is a natural expression found in a garden home. Creating these "setups" for easy rotation is important because unless you are using evergreens or sedums, you're likely to want to change blooming plants with the seasons. Having a few anchoring plants that serve as a constant in the design with only an occasional change-out makes this process easy and pleasurable. I use a wide range of containers to hold garden plants and accents—everything from baskets, troughs, and wooden window boxes to galvanized buckets hung from brackets. And don't overlook your porch railing as a place to securely anchor a box of blooms.

beauty in a box

Window boxes filled with soil and plants are heavy, so for safety's sake, be sure the box is securely fastened below the windowsill. To attach a window box on brackets, fasten the brackets to the framework of the window 4 inches from each end of the box. Use hardware and fasteners that won't rust, such as brass, stainless steel, or galvanized or coated iron. Look for special rail hangers to safely secure a planter box on a railing, but first check the railing to be sure it is also strong and not wobbly.

Above: These cold-hardy plants, including 'Golden Ingot' ivy, 'Mahagony' ajuga, 'Emerald Gaiety' wintercreeper, 'Nagoya' and 'Dynasty' ornamental kale, Mediterranean heather, and bloody dock, make a colorful fall display. **Left:** Caladiums, impatiens, variegated liriope, and variegated airplane plant (*Chlorophytum comosum* 'Vittatum') brighten this shady spot on the porch. **Opposite:** A moss-filled wire basket serves as a window box planter for the wildflower-style blooms of 'Big Sky Sundown' coneflower.

4. Recast Roles

We all are learning ways to recycle, reuse, and reduce. Having been raised with grandparents who never forgot the travails of the Great Depression, the idea of reusing things was imprinted on me and my siblings at an early age. I heard the phrase "Never throw anything away; you may need it someday" repeated so often that it seems to be part of my DNA. However, as my friends like to remind me whenever they see my garage, this habit has its limits. But I'm quick to point out that a modified version of this philosophy can be useful, particularly when repurposing items to serve as plant holders. It's a fun and creative way to add a touch of whimsy to an entrance. Anything goes! An old coal grate can serve as a container for enthusiastic bloomers, and a chair with a worn-out bottom can be transformed into a holder for a pot of plants. Use your imagination to create innovative ways to display bounty from the garden.

Opposite: The friendly mini-petunia-sized blossoms of 'Superbells Red' calibrachoa bubble out from the top of the old cast-iron coal grate. Heavy containers like this are ideal for outdoor settings, as they stay well anchored in high winds and can take extremes in weather.

FLORAL FOAM TIP

Craft stores sell blocks of floral foam that can be cut, soaked, and placed in containers as a base to arrange flowers. Always soak the foam in a bucket or bowl filled with fresh water, not under the tap. Simply drop the foam onto the water and let it take up the moisture naturally. Don't try to weight it down. When the top of the foam is level with the surface of the water, remove it and allow it to drain. Oversoaking causes the foam to break up in use.

Using bags or sacks as plant holders can be a fun and surprising choice that is sure to draw some attention. The key to arranging branches in a porous holder is to bundle together the stems of the plants, stick them into a block of floral foam, and place the foam in a plastic watertight bag. Fill the bag with enough water to cover the foam before sealing it with a heavy-duty rubber band. Carefully slide the bagged end of the plant down the opening of the sack. The water in the bags will keep the plants fresh and the floral foam will help keep the stems from piercing the bag. To add more water, loosen the rubber band and use a turkey baster to replenish the plastic bag.

Get creative and try other types of holders. I've used wooden shoes to hold eggs, boots (my old green Wellies) to display cut branches, and long stockings attached to walls filled with greenery, flowers, and berries.

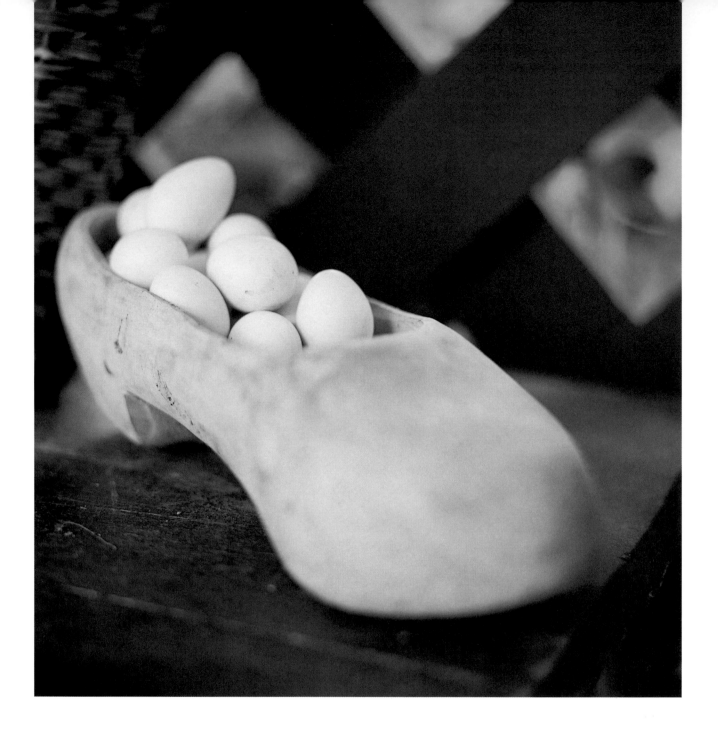

Above: A wooden shoe makes a temporary holder for some recently gathered chicken eggs. **Opposite:** Next to the cabin's back door on the screen porch a canvas bag serves as the container for cut boughs from a flowering smooth sumac. The bench along the wall displays homemade punched tin candle holders and a wooden log planter with Japanese painted fern, 'Dolce Mocha Mint' heuchera, 'Opal Innocence' nemesia, and 'Catalina Blue' torenia.

converted containers *(be sure to add drainage holes)*

Galvanized tub	Wheelbarrow	Giant seashell
Hat	Fruit crate	Canning jar
Cup	Kitchen crock / canisters	Wooden bushel basket
Old dresser drawer	Discarded porcelain sink	Discarded outdoor grill
Stovepipe	Mixing bowl	Wastebasket

collections | BEGONIAS

It is probably no surprise that I have many friends who have carried plant collecting about as far as is humanly possible. What started as a hobby for some has grown into a commercial enterprise. Some of these enterprises have become so colossal in size that I am sure my friends would never have imagined their hobby growing to such a scale the day they first laid eyes on the plant that is now at the center of their careers. Orchid growers would have to rank at the top of the list of collectors, but there are others who have become collectors of zonal geraniums, African violets, succulents of all kinds, and certainly begonias.

While I doubt my preoccupation with the begonia will ever result in a major commercial venture, I do gather them whenever I find a cache of unique varieties. As we often are, early in my years of plant collecting, I was attracted to a plant's bloom, but that soon gave way to my admiration of foliage. It is here where begonias really shine. Seeing the breadth of foliage is like a visit to the fabric store. Some leaves have "seersucker puckers" while others are smooth as silk.

You can also find the foliage with stripes and polka dots. And the colors of the leaves actually have a broader range of hues than the blooms: cream or chocolate, with silvery and metallic highlights.

My potting shed is full of begonia varieties. They seem to thrive there in the bright filtered light and moderate temperatures. My current favorites include several of the rex begonia hybrids grown for their electrifying foliage—'Escarole', 'Palomar Prince', 'Taurus', 'Cherries and Chocolate', 'Miami Storm', and 'Fireflush'. I also adore the old angel wings that adorned our grandmothers' porches and I'm pleased that some of these have been hybridized to perform robustly in landscapes. One of these is the popular 'Dragonwing' series of begonias with glossy foliage and flowers in pink, red, or white. Another one that I grew outdoors with great success was an older angel wing hybrid called 'Sinbad'. I was particularly attracted to its silvery leaves and pink pendulous flowers. It was so gorgeous in containers and such a good bedfellow with the ferns, heucheras, and impatiens in my shade garden that I look forward to using it again this year.

5. Elevate a Collection

A seasoned interior designer once passed along a couple of his tricks-of-the-trade that I've always found useful in my garden designs. The first piece of advice was that some things just need a bit of a lift to be noticed. And the other was that similar objects have more visual impact when grouped together. I've used both of these tips to good effect in the garden. For instance, when planting a flower bed, I place taller plants in the back of the border and shorter ones in the front. This elevates the plants that are more than an arm's length away to a height that brings them closer to the eye. And by planting a large block of the same plants together, they appear as a bold splash of color rather than small dots through the garden.

Try these tips when assembling an arrangement at the entrance of your home. Raise your display off the ground so it will be noticed. I use whatever I have on hand to elevate a collection and then I group similar objects or plants together. It's a simple but effective way of bringing the area to life and turning even the smallest of spaces into a mini-world of its own.

Below: While the plants on the table are all begonias, the variety and color in the leaves provide enough contrast to make them an eye-catching display. All these begonias enjoy filtered light and consistent moisture. When selecting a group of plants to display together, make sure they all need the same type of growing conditions so they will thrive.

plant elevators

Bench	Plinths	Stack of bricks
Table	Half columns	Stump of wood
Stools	Overturned containers	Stepladder

6. Keep Props Handy

Make it easy to adorn your entrance by keeping a few support pieces in place such as a small table, wide-mouthed bottles, baskets, and some containers. You'll be more likely to notice and fill your entryway with things you gather when these support pieces are close at hand. These basic pieces also make it easy to modify the composition without spending a lot of time and energy. They needn't be elaborate. In the summer, I leave a few French flower market cans by the back step as ready receptacles for bundles of cut flowers. When filled with armloads of flowers, they make a colorful display until I'm ready to use them in an arrangement inside.

What applies to the outside can also be applied indoors as well. Create similar compositions just inside the door as a place for seasonal accents as you leave the house. When considering where to put your efforts and energy, focus on the places you see and use every day and keep a few carefully chosen pieces that are functional, decorative, or preferably both.

Above Right: Purple pansies and the silvery foliage of dusty miller fill a hanging basket. A moss-lined wire basket of 'Valerie Finnis' grape hyacinths and the variegated leaves of flax lily echo the purple, white, and green color theme. **Right:** Freshly picked bundles of sunflowers, gomphrena, celosia, and Mexican sage give the entry a flower-market feel. **Opposite:** My collection of rex begonia is taking over much of my lathe house. Since these begonias require more humidity than others during warm weather, I often hose down the gravel on the floor, and as the water evaporates it cools the air and adds humidity. To bring out the beautiful colors on the leaves I keep the plants out of direct sunlight.

7. *Create Harmony with Similar Containers*

Years ago I discovered that one way to pull together an eclectic composition is to introduce a single mediating element. Since then, I've used this lesson to good effect both inside and out. For instance, inside I have a large collection of family and friends' photos that I like to display on a side table. Some of the pictures are black-and-white photographs taken years ago and others are more recent color prints from trips and events. When I set them out on the table to choose which photos to use they were all so different that they didn't really hang together as a group. Some are close-ups of one person and others are wide shots taken of a group of people. They recall great memories and I enjoy looking at them so I wanted to find a way to make them feel like a collection. The answer was to put them all in silver frames. That's what was needed to unify them as a tabletop display. Not all of the frames are identical. Some are taller than others, and some have an embossed design, but the material, style, and silvery color is similar enough to unite the arrangement.

I carry the same approach into creating displays just outside the door. When I put together an arrangement of plants next to an entrance, I often pull together those with different forms, shapes, and colors so the qualities of each one stand out and can be appreciated for their own merits. But without some unifying element, the plants look like a random selection that lacks harmony. Much like the frames around the photos, displaying the plants in containers made from the same material or a similar color, such as terra-cotta or glazed or galvanized ceramic, transforms what at first may look like unrelated elements into a collection. The disparate, often clashing colors or varied textures in plants are unified by this simple strategy. Grounding the would-be chaos in the "sameness" can help to synchronize the display. And just like the frames, the containers need not be the same in size or form, but when they are made from the same material and color, a cohesive effect is achieved.

Opposite: Blue containers in various shapes and sizes act to unify this collection of tropical plants. The bold leaves of 'Illustris' elephant ear (*Colocasia esculenta*) create a backdrop for the square container filled with umbrella plant (*Cyperus alternifolius*) and cascading 'Goldilocks' creeping Jenny (*Lysimachia nummularia* 'Goldilocks') next to 'Ogon' sweet flag (*Acorus gramineus* 'Ogan') and a dish container of rosette-style sedums (*Echeveria*).

8. Display Your Finds

When considering ways to add a garden-home flavor to your interior decor, broaden your definition beyond plants to include a variety of natural items. During my travels and even on walks through the garden, I often collect and bring in all kinds of little treasures I pick up along the way. I use the mantel of my fireplace in the front hall to display many of my finds. Old glass vases contain some of these items but for the most part, I like to arrange the objects alongside one another across the mantel. They are a mix of curiosities: many are simply interesting rocks or shells that caught my eye. Some are relics from the past, such as the tiny third-century terra-cotta head of a goddess from Turkey, arrowheads, and a piece of petrified wood from North Dakota (thirty million years old), while others have personal meaning, such as a feather collection gathered from my own flock of domestic poultry and from wild birds alike. I have many tiny bronze sculptures and pieces of Old Paris porcelain mixed in with the found objects.

BARGAINING POWER

When you're on the hunt in antiques stores, yard sales, or flea markets for something to add to your collections and you want to see if there is any room for negotiation, start the conversation by saying, "Could you give me your best price for this?"

Most of what is displayed is valuable only to me. I like the way they all hang together, although every time they need dusting, I think they should be issued into a proper curio cabinet, but I like them casually displayed and out where I can see them. Use the area just inside your entry to reveal a little bit about yourself. Even if you don't have a Monticello-size foyer, use the area to create your own display objects special to you.

Opposite: While furniture, carpet, and drapes all contribute to the style and look of a room, without the addition of personal objects, the space can feel stark and lifeless. There are no rules to arranging these items other than what pleases your eye. Think of them as still-life arrangements, but keep them fresh by reinventing the displays with new treasures. The large mirror above my mantel allows for a 360-degree view of the objects.

It's hard for me to recall when I first started collecting Paris porcelain vases. There are so many in my collection that the occasion of purchasing my first one has now blurred in my mind. While they are not as ubiquitous or as affordable as they once were, I still find them from time to time, if I'm lucky, underpriced and sitting slightly out of view alone and forlorn in junk shops.

Most of my vases are well worn and have only a trace of the gold that once adorned them, but many still have their colored decorations intact. These motifs can range from simple bouquets and arrangements of flora to more elaborate designs. Often they depict Arcadian scenes or classical landscapes. Others celebrate agrarian icons (with cartouches of farm implements and the bounty of the harvest), images, and figures from classical mythology. I often marvel at the artistry applied to these vases, each hand-painted, thereby making them unique expressions. The shapes of the vases are as varied as the paintings on them. Many must have been produced as pairs for mantel garniture or to accent the top of a chest of drawers in a bedroom, but most of mine are single vases, having lost their mates sometime in the distant past.

I use them regularly as vessels to hold whatever might be coming into prominence in the garden, whether it is fruit, foliage, or flower. I am particularly fond of certain pieces and use them for special occasions. For instance, a favorite vase for the Thanksgiving season is one I found in a shop in Texarkana (a town on the border of Texas and Arkansas). The colors are perfect for an autumn display.

Others are best used to display fresh blooms when my old-fashioned rose collection is in full show the first week of May. To my eye, the clean white porcelain with its touches of color and bits of gold seem the perfect complement to my heirloom roses. And the more chips, cracks, and worn the vase, the more at home and at ease the roses seem to be. I'm sure this compatibility is no accident when you realize that many of the old-rose varieties we grow are French in origin and come from the same time period as the porcelain (first quarter of the nineteenth century). Many of my roses reflect that heritage in their names—'Madame Plantier', 'Souvenir de la Malmaison', 'Lamarque', and 'Madame Alfred Carrière', to cite just a few. We have the patronage of Napoléon's Joséphine for the proliferation of so many sweetly scented rose introductions and the artisans of Paris for such inspired vessels to display them in.

9. *Refocus Attention*

Have you ever noticed when you place an object on a table or a picture on the wall that after a while, it becomes part of the overall decor of a room and you don't really "see" it anymore? One of the reasons to bring elements of the garden inside is to draw fresh attention to certain objects and renew our view of areas that have become stagnant. Plants seem to carry with them a different energy and can set into motion a dynamic among various elements in an area that stimulates us. The next time you enter a room for the first time, notice how you look around until you see something that grabs your attention. With something to focus on, you begin to take in the surrounding objects. A bouquet of flowers often serves as a fresh focal point to capture our attention and then directs us to see what's next to it. To measure this effect, bring in a bouquet of flowers and place them in a simple glass container. Move the arrangement around the room to assess the impact it makes. Notice how it draws attention to the object next to it.

Experiment with different locations until you find the place where it belongs. Along with being a point of beauty, blossoms help soften the hard lines of objects and the architecture of our interior spaces. The delicate petals of a flower act as a visual foil next to a sculpture or inanimate object. It doesn't take much—just a little foliage or a few blooms can transform a space.

TAKE A PICTURE

Photograph the area where you want to create a display. Digital cameras make this easy and fun. Once you create your arrangement, photograph the area again. You'll be amazed at how this gives you a fresh perspective on what is needed and if your arrangement is successful.

Opposite: A houseplant or bouquet in contrasting colors placed near an object on a table helps to draw the eye to an overlooked area. Fresh-cut flowering boughs of white rhododendrons draw attention to the blue ceramic plate on this side table. By keeping the flower arrangement the same height and size as the plate, the blooms don't overwhelm the art, but work with it to create a still-life arrangement.

10. Mix Mediums

In the days before digital photography, I was touring some historic gardens in England and mistakenly put a roll of black-and-white film in my camera instead of color. When I opened the packet of developed pictures, I was so disappointed that I tossed them in a drawer of my desk without really looking at them. Then one day, as I was straightening things, I picked them up and noticed something unexpected. With the color drained from the scenes, a fascinating component of the garden's design was revealed. I began to see an underlying beauty in the way the shapes, textures, and patterns of the garden's design had been arranged.

Since then, whether I'm designing a garden or creating a "tablescape" inside my house, I often try to step back and imagine how the scene would look in black and white. This exercise helps me see beyond color to create compelling displays. Indoors, I've found a combination of the natural and the man-made, the old and new, gathered and purchased makes intriguing studies that stamp a room with personal style. As you create displays inside your entry, think about pairing opposites: hard and soft, nubby and smooth, rough and slick, fuzzy and silky, coarse and fine. Mix things up and experiment with your objects. Earthy textures enliven inanimate elements and help define a room's mood. When planning your mix, pick the atmosphere you want and rely on items that express that feeling for a majority of the display, and then look for ways in which to throw in some diversity for more interest.

Above: A diminutive third-century terra-cotta head of a goddess from Turkey is displayed next to a mercury-glass vase. **Left:** The colors and patterns of seashells are appreciated in this fluted vase.
Opposite: The earthy texture of the ceramic jar filled with boughs from my maple tree act as a foil to the classical marble bust. Intermixed in the display are the striking flowers of the butterfly amaryllis 'Papilio', the emerging blooms of paperwhites, a bronze bird statue, and some long-abandoned nests.

11. *Play Plants Off Containers*

When choosing the type of vase or container to use in displaying plants, I often go for something that adds a contrasting element to the design. For instance, dark objects have the quality of anchoring the more ephemeral. In certain situations this grounding force can help set the mood you want. A dark-colored object or even one with mass and texture that can communicate visual weight can act as a foil to the light airy stems of winter twigs, forsythia, quince, and flowering branches. The vessel then helps to draw our attention to what otherwise would be too diaphanous to recognize. At the same time, when the plant is visually strong in its own right, a container such as a wire basket or a clear vase is a good choice, so it doesn't compete for attention.

One of my favorite restaurants in New York is Gramercy Park Tavern. I often have admired their displays that include the use of seasonal branches in dramatic and effective ways. Vast bundles of limbs emerge out of rustic containers and blend with the ambience of the space in a way that allows the branches to deliver the punch. Arrangements on tables on either side of your entry can be used to convey that same sense of style.

Right: A wire basket holds a collection of colorful foliage plants, including Italian stone pine, 'Fire Power' nandina, 'Glacier' ivy, and 'Black Scallop' bugleweed. To protect the table, the basket is lined with moss and then lined with a plastic liner before the soil and plants were added.

TRANSPORTING FLOWERS

To keep a vase of cut flowers from tipping over in a car while you are driving, try this: Fill the container with just a few inches of water and place it in a cooler. Encircle the base of the vase with weighty objects such as stones or bricks and then fill in the rest of the cooler with crumpled newspapers.

collections | BASKETS

Baskets are indispensable in the garden home. The myriad shapes, sizes, weaves, and styles make them handy to have around for an inexhaustible number of reasons. Since there are examples from every culture, there are baskets for every decorating style, even the most formal. You often see large willow baskets filled with firewood next to the firebox in an English country home's drawing room. The contrast of these handmade, rustic objects next to a seventeenth-century Italian mantelpiece is an exciting juxtaposition.

One of my favorite baskets that I use regularly is one I bought when I was a student in England. As part of the garden-history course, we often went on field trips to estates. It didn't take long for me to catch on that carrying my lunch and snacks in plastic bags did little to endear me to some of my more style-conscious classmates. So I found a small picnic hamper at Habitat, Terence Conran's posh shop in London. Once fitted with my oilcloth jacket, Wellies, and basket, I was ready for any outing.

I reach for baskets regularly when integrating the garden into the home. By simply lining them with a plastic bag, they can contain most of what I might suddenly decide to display in them.

12. Exhibit the Season

Just as outdoor entries are ideal spots to create seasonal displays, tables in foyers are also perfect locations for arrangements that reflect the time of the year. I love to greet guests with the brilliance of botanical elements as they cross the threshold to come inside. Whether it is a shock of brilliant yellow flowering forsythia branches in an urn on the center table, or twisting vines of bitter-sweet and fall gourds casually strewn over the top of a chest, staging the scene with decorative accents from nature carries that sense of the garden inside.

SEASONAL SENSIBILITIES

Keep pace with the natural world in your interior accents by modifying your displays with the seasons. Re-create the sensual qualities of nature by selecting items with wonderful aromas, interesting textures, and tactile qualities that capture that time of year.

Opposite: This happy bouquet of large cupped and tazetta daffodils contains a few of the varieties I grow. If you'd like some of these carefree flowers in your garden, plant the bulbs in the fall, and the following spring they will emerge in a bright array of blooms. Cut the flowers and leave the foliage to recharge the bulb and you'll enjoy a return performance the following spring.

Certainly plants are an indication of a particular season, but objects also name their place. Mixing them together creates a three-dimensional still-life. It's easy to forget that the items we collect may also suggest a time of the year. But if you pause to think about it, many objects imply a season by virtue of the time of the year they are most often used or the colors, patterns, or textures they possess. Bright green dishware suggests spring, crocks used in canning and food preparation remind us of late summer, antique toys most likely were gifts given to children during the holidays. When you look at your collections this way, they can be combined with botanical accents from that same season to create a more layered, eclectic look. For instance, I have a collection of old harvesting hand tools that make lively accents for autumn displays along with gourds, sun-flowers, and ornamental grasses. In spring galvanized buckets and watering cans with a collection of spring-flowering bulbs has a similar expressive effect. And in summer, an item from my collection of antique flower frogs, along with a wooden garden trug, seems a fitting companion for fresh produce and flowers that reflect the abundance of the garden. In winter I like to add sparkle and brightness to the entry by placing glass and crystal objects near candelabras and lanterns to capture and reflect the light. Adorned with greenery, pinecones, and berried boughs, the mix of color and shine is quite appealing. Consider recasting some of your collections into seasonal displays.

Paperwhites in a Glass Container

When paperwhites bloom they can become top heavy and need a little support. By planting the bulbs in a tall glass container, the flowers are held upright and the fragrance floats out of the top.

Decorative stones or pebbles	4–5 paperwhite bulbs
Large glass vase 24 inches or taller	Water

1. Add just enough decorative stones to the vase to keep the paperwhites upright and out of water and to give visual weight to the container. Take 4–5 paperwhites (or whatever the vase will accommodate) and nestle them among the stones with the growing tip pointed up. Add a few more stones if necessary to hold them in place.

2. Add enough water to the vase so that the bases of the bulbs are getting moisture to stimulate root growth but the rest of the bulb is not submerged. Check every week to see if more water is needed.

3. Expect flowers in 3 to 6 weeks, depending on the temperature and light. Plants grow in normal household conditions with bright light being supplied when foliage begins to emerge from the bulbs.

Done!

Tip: *For a shortcut, buy pots of paperwhites already growing at nurseries or garden centers. Once home, rinse the sand or soil off the bulbs, and then place the plants in the vase and anchor the bulbs with stones.*

13. Use Gray to Harmonize

The longer I garden, the more I appreciate the color gray. It plays a unique role in developing a successful color scheme in flower gardens. Gray's soft demeanor is poised somewhere between black and white, with just a hint of all of nature's colors mixed in. This chameleon-like quality helps it to act as a harmonizing agent between hues that would otherwise clash if they were placed next to one another. No matter what colors are laid on either side, gray contains just enough of each hue that it blends with both, mediating the mix.

I've often used gray foliage plants in the garden to give the eye a visual break between contrasting colors or even completely different color themes. In large areas where I like to punctuate long stretches of flower borders with combinations of plants, silvery-colored leaves are particularly useful. The foliage acts to cleanse the visual palate much like a sip of water or a bite of bread gives the taste buds a break when wine tasting. It is such a low-key color it doesn't grab our attention but when you look around, it is woven into the tapestry of much of the landscape including bark, stones, and even the sky on overcast days.

Gray is really too simple a word to describe the color of most of these plants, inasmuch as there are many gradations of color, ranging from a silver that fairly sparkles in the afternoon light to a flatter tone that verges on blue. Gray foliage in plants is attractive, even in the harsh, flat light of noon, when most greens lose the richness and yellows and white become too intense. There is a "roundness" to the color that adds a soothing quality to the garden.

PROTECT CONCRETE

If you plan on using concrete ornaments or pots outside, they may need some help to withstand the winter. Since concrete is semi-porous, water can get into small areas, then freeze and expand, causing the item to chip and break. For added protection, follow label directions and apply a clear concrete sealer to the surface.

So it's no wonder I turn to gray inside the house to serve the same role as it does in the garden. My back-door entry is a hodgepodge of coats, hats, bags, and dropped-off items in a kaleidoscope of colors. By adding a collection of calm, gray stone and concrete containers and statues, there is a break between the items hung on the wall and those that reside on the counter. Although the collection of gray stoneware is quite different in form, the gray color lets them all hang together in complete harmony. And to keep the arrangement from becoming too serious, I loosen it up by adding plants and using the stone cherubs as a hat rack.

Opposite: The rubbery leaves of an echeveria, a rosette-forming succulent that is native from Mexico to northwestern South America, fill the square concrete container. The urn is planted with an aloe vera, another type of succulent. The fleshy, thick leaves and strong forms of these plants are a good match for the concrete ornaments.

collections | CONCRETE ORNAMENTS

When I was a kid growing up in the rural South every farmer's wife had some type of concrete garden ornament on her lawn; swan planters were predictable at each side of the drive entrance, as were white hens with the occasional bright yellow chicks. Sadly, I think the chicks were often lost to the lawn mower. And, of course, there were always the lawn jockeys and gnomes in need of paint along with the ubiquitous birdbath surrounded in a bed of red salvia and marigolds. These concrete objects were given new life with a fresh coat of paint usually when fences were whitewashed or the barns repainted. It seems when new, they came in a variety of colors, but over time they became monochromatic with repeated latherings of white paint.

Today, these little chunks of Americana fetch surprising prices in antiques and garden shops. Even with missing limbs and other evidence of wear and tear, they have found their way inside as interior accessories, particularly in homes going for a cottage look or shabby chic.

I find many of these objects useful both inside and outside the house. And when on the lookout for them, I don't limit my selection to concrete; really, anything that resembles that look, stone or even plaster, will catch my eye. I admit I lean toward those that are more distressed than new. If I find something that looks too new, I knock it around a bit with a chain or hand tool, then give it a good grunging with a haphazard application of a green/gray paint that is brushed on and rubbed off. There is, however, nothing quite like the patina of time and a hard life to give an object character.

14. Keep the Eye Occupied

Just inside my front door is a round mahogany table that serves as a kind of a catchall where I can toss my keys, stack books, and create an eye-pleasing display. I enjoy changing the arrangement occasionally, but when I'm traveling I find it's hard to keep up with the maintenance of cut flowers. So one week I decided to pot a mix of plants that would last while I was away. In digging around the cupboard for a decorative container, I spied a large silver serving bowl that was the perfect size for the table. The bowl inspired me to create an arrangement of plants that would play off the bowl's glossy surface. As I chose the plants to use, I was reminded of the time I was designing an all-white garden for the north side of my house. When I began I thought there wouldn't be much to it; all I needed to do was fill the beds with plants that had gray or silver foliage or white flowers. I soon discovered it wasn't quite that simple. I found that when designing a monochromatic color scheme it's important to combine plants that have contrasting shapes, textures, and patterns so they don't all blur together. When there was some distinguishing difference between the plants, each would visually hold its own area and be appreciated. So the challenge was to find the right combinations.

The same principle applies when decorating inside. When objects of similar colors are displayed next to one another, it is the difference in their shape, texture, and pattern that provides visual interest. In the garden, or in the house, when you take the time to look beyond the bloom of a plant, you begin to see all kinds of qualities you might otherwise miss, such as its outline or form. Some plants are upright while others are cascading. The texture of the leaves can vary a great deal, from fuzzy to glossy. And many plants have variegated patterns on their leaves. Look for these contrasts and try your hand at creating your own version of a monochromatic display.

Above: A silver bowl holds a silvery blend of plants, including 'Calico' variegated ivy, 'Icicles' licorice plant, 'Silver Dragon' lilyturf, 'Emerald Gaiety' euonymus, 'Suffruticosa' English boxwood, and two varieties of ornamental kale, 'White Dynasty' and 'White Peacock'.

15. Be a Mimic of Nature

The next time you are in a natural area, notice the way Mother Nature plants her garden. She often uses a wide paintbrush to create large drifts of the same variety of plants. Rarely will you find a plant isolated by itself, or dotted here and there throughout an area. More often several of the same plant grow in colonies or clusters. The result is a dramatic display that fills the landscape with a sweep of color and a bold presence. It's a lesson worth learning. After all, who can argue with the best floral designer in the business?

Sometimes it's fun to create a stylized version of nature's plan. Both indoors and out, I often cluster a number of the same plants together to give an arrangement more visual impact. When applying this idea to dried displays, there are some other factors to consider. Since the plants often have more muted hues than fresh-cut blooms, I look for material with intriguing textures and bold forms to give the display some added punch.

After watching my flower beds fill with 'Purple Sensation' alliums, and enjoying the blossoms filled with hundreds of tiny violet-purple flowers compressed into gorgeous round balls on 36-inch stems, I decided to dry the flowers so I could create a version of the design indoors. I cut the stems at the ground and hung them in a cool dry place until the flower balls dried to a creamy light brown. Then small holes where drilled in a wooden base so the single stems of the dried blooms could be staged to look as if they were still growing in the garden. The resulting arrangement showcases the vertical qualities of alliums and makes a sculptural display for a side table in an entry.

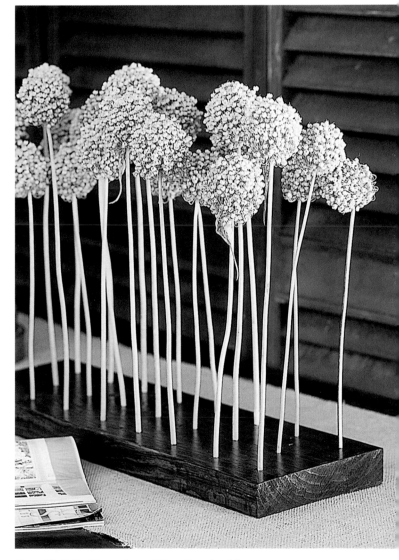

Above: To air-dry blooms, harvest them throughout the growing season when they look their best. Strip the leaves and hang large flowers, such as alliums or hydrangeas, individually upside-down in a warm, well-ventilated place out of direct sunlight. Bundle smaller flowers together by wrapping a handful of stems together with a rubber band.

16. Bridge the Gap

Entries are sometimes decorated with pictures and wall-hugging furnishings, so there is open floor space near the door where people can freely move as they enter and exit. Between the top surface of the furniture and the bottom edge of the art, there is often a gap separating the two elements. To add a sense of connection between them, add a touch of the garden. In these places, I often rely on a low-maintenance houseplant or seasonal objects that can be easily changed.

Plants are useful in mediating the area between art and furniture because you can select the container and the shape of the plant to either repeat the forms above and below it or add a contrasting element. Here, a rectangular trunk is connected to a framed picture by a similarly shaped planter full of sedum. Using a plant to fill in the space between furniture and a picture on the wall unifies them in a cohesive arrangement.

just inside the door

Historically, the area called the entry or foyer just inside the doorway played an occasional ceremonial role in welcoming people. It has also served as an area to display a variety of objects. Thomas Jefferson used his grand entrance hall at Monticello to showcase the famous calendar clock he invented as well as his maps, busts, and a variety of natural history specimens such as antlers and bones. To accommodate his many visitors, the room contained up to twenty-eight chairs.

In Victorian times the foyer was the place guests and gentleman callers waited patiently as their name cards were presented on silver trays to the hosts and hostesses. These days, not many of us keep our guests cooling their heels in the entryway. But that doesn't mean that the foyer has lost its sense of drama. The area can still be a place to display favorite things, greet guests, and combine the beauty of the home and nature.

Opposite: Elevated to table height, the wooden chest has more of a presence in the entry. Its shape and form serve as a counterbalance to the artwork on the wall. To help unify the design, a simple container that echoes the rectangular shape of the chest and the picture frame is placed on top of the trunk. The round leaves of the plant in the container also mirror the swirling patterns found in the art piece. These repeating forms create a sense of continuity in the arrangement.

17. Encourage Touch

Those who garden can easily describe the many ways the activity engages all of their senses. Not only is it a place of visual delight, but it also draws us into a relationship with nature grounded in touch, taste, smell, and sound: the way soil crumbles in the hand, the taste of summer's first tomato, the smell of newly mown grass, or the sound of a thin stream of water moving over stones. When elements that enhance our sensual experiences are added to our home's interior decor, those objects serve as portals reconnecting us to those primal experiences. The space becomes a much richer and relaxing environment.

But it must be said that for many of us to be able to add this layer of heightened sensuality, we must first overcome some often-repeated messages we may have heard as children. From my youngest years, one of the last things that my mother would say to me as I turned the doorknob to enter a shop with expensive glassware, or when the family was visiting someone's house, was "Don't touch anything!" That admonition still rings in my head, but to me there are some things that are so beautiful and engaging that the only way to truly experience them is through touch. I find a home without the textures of nature to be a rather flat and soulless place.

Opposite: Two main colors unify this display—green and brown. The electrifying chartreuse of the Osage orange fruits and the lemon cypress tree along with the bronze brown hues of the containers and water-hose nozzles create a compelling arrangement, but it is the display's intriguing textures that make it so irresistible: feathery and soft, rubbery and wrinkled, smooth and well worn. Together they provide a tantalizing array of tactile surfaces.

MORE THAN PLANTS

Perhaps the simplest way to create garden style is to move outdoor items to an indoor room. Adirondack chairs and a weathered bench are perfectly employable in a living room. Retired garden tools, buckets and gates, floral fabrics, aged wood, botanical prints, bark-covered lamps, smooth stones, and bamboo shades are other elements that bring a sense of the garden inside.

The tactile quality of natural items can sway the mood of a room. Areas that have angular and rigid lines are immediately changed with objects that entice you to reach out and touch them. Soft furnishing such as curtains, pillows, and throws offer that same atmosphere-changing effect. Just inside the entry is a great spot for creating a sensual accent. You can immediately signal whether yours is a home to kick off your shoes and get comfortable or a place to sit on the edge of a chair with hands carefully folded.

In this arrangement, the soft plumelike foliage of a lemon cypress tree and the bumpy texture of the Osage orange fruit piled in the bowl create a tactile display that is hard to resist. A collection of antique water-hose spigots adds another layer of touchable interest. The aim of adding garden-home elements isn't to achieve the impersonal prettiness of a showcase room but to create an expressive space that reflects your interests, tastes, and personality.

Everyone seems naturally drawn to the kitchen and dining room. That's certainly true in my home. Whenever friends and family gather, they seem to gravitate to these areas. As the hub of the house, the kitchen and dining room serve many daily needs. They also carry symbolic weight as the place to share activities and meals among familiar objects and friendly faces.

For me, enjoying food prepared with fresh produce is one of my garden's best rewards. A close second is embellishing the kitchen and dining room with seasonal displays. Necessities aside, whether I am preparing a meal or sitting down to dine, I like to decorate these high-profile rooms with the things that have meaning to me.

It's the perfect place to combine objects from my dishware, silver, and art collections with plants from the garden.

Just as my garden designs are visually layered, so, too, is the decor in my kitchen and dining room. The dining room is just off the kitchen with several pieces of American Empire furniture that I've collected since I first set up my household. Most of the handmade pieces date to the early 1800s and are characterized by their simple, massive, yet graceful curves in dark mahogany and veneers.

To balance the bulk of the furniture, I echoed a color scheme from one of my garden hollies (*Ilex opaca* 'Carolina No. 2'). I've always considered the American holly to be one of the noblest trees in the southeastern forest. It holds a special place in my memory as I recall its prominent evergreen foliage standing against the winter landscape on visits to my family in Tennessee. If you take a close look at fully ripened holly berries you will find they are such an intense shade of red that they almost appear to glow.

I borrowed the holly's red-and-green colors to use in the dining room but modified their tonal qualities. To offset the dark brownish red shades of the furniture, I chose a mint green wall color. For the floor, rather than add more pattern to the room, I covered the red pine wood with a durable sisal rug. Its sandy brown color and woven texture add an organic feel. The idea was to create a background of fairly neutral colors to allow the furnishings and accessories to pop.

Opposite, clockwise from top left: On special occasions I enjoy lighting the candles and laying out a feast, both for the eyes and the taste buds; the more elegant the table setting, the simpler I like to make the garden-inspired accents, such as these serving pieces piled with golden bronze pears that pick up the colors in the plates and room decor. Simple and bold, this centerpiece displays a series of rounded forms including the bowl of the silver epergne, the golden pears, and the ball-shaped boxwoods with a circle of lighted votives. The narrow-necked antique water bottles are stored on the lower shelf of my lion-pawed American Empire pier table; the mirror set between the back legs of the table reflects the sparkle from the bottles. The shy, nodding blooms of summer snowflakes create a simple and appealing display; a handful of blooms in several narrow-neck glass water bottles highlight their long beautiful stems.

18. Pick Up the Pace

In both garden and interior design, repeating the same element three times or more can have a powerful effect. Whether it is columns regularly spaced along the front of a porch or matching bouquets of flowers on a counter, a cadence is established by lining up a series of the same objects. By repeating colors, patterns, or shapes, you can create a visual rhythm that grabs your attention and leads the eye through a room.

As you select flowers for this kind of arrangement, be aware that the visual pace of the display will be affected by the overall shape of the bouquets and the spacing between the containers. For example, rounded forms, such as bundles of daffodils placed some distance apart, set a softer, more languid pace than closely spaced bouquets of flowers with straight stalks that create a sharper, staccato look. Putting these arrangements together is easily accomplished when you have a multitude of the same flowers in bloom such as daffodils and tulips in spring, zinnias in summer, or bundles of colorful leaves in autumn. The bolder and brighter the colors, the more noticeable they become.

Above right: A regular tempo is established in this simple arrangement by using all-white African violets in similar containers spaced equally along the top of the rustic bench. The two pink pots between the three yellow containers are like high notes in the melody. **Opposite:** Three identical golden globes of daffodil blossoms in simple square glass containers punctuate the marble top of the sideboard in my kitchen. The bouquets are low enough as to not interfere with the display on the wall, but large enough to lead the eye across the room.

DAFFODILS DON'T MIX WELL WITH OTHERS
Cut daffodils exude a sticky sap that clouds the water and clogs the stems of other cut flowers. Woody branches such as cut forsythia and quince are not as quickly affected as the hollow, succulent stems of tulips and other flowers. Avoid using daffodils in mixed flower bouquets.

19. *Bring Bedding Plants Indoors*

By the time spring rolls around, I'm more than eager to fill my flower beds with color. By March, I've had my fill of brown grass and bare branches, so I'm ready to see some green in the garden. I usually go a little crazy at the nursery and buy all the plants my car will carry. Once I arrive home, I spread out all the plants on the lawn so I can admire my new treasures and then use the area as a staging ground until I can get them all planted. It's a spring ritual that I'm compelled to perform each year. I can only imagine the glee my local garden center owner must feel when he sees me drive up. When my family owned a garden center, I would have been just the kind of customer that I looked forward to see: someone with a passion for plants and who had lots of room in his car to haul things home!

A few years ago, I was going through this seasonal rite of passage and was about to plant a few containers by the back door. I'd been at it since dawn, so I walked into the kitchen to grab a cup of coffee when suddenly the thought hit me: Why not pot a few of the annual bedding plants into some dishware to create an indoor centerpiece? Think about it—those little guys come to us already loaded with color and packed into tiny cell packs with more blooms per square inch than you can imagine. So I grabbed some sweet-faced violas and popped them into a white-scalloped serving dish I had in my cupboard. I choose violas because they do well in low light and will stay perky and fresh for several days. In the garden, I plant lots of them to brighten my borders in early spring because they can take a frost and keep right on blooming. After enjoying the results of my impromptu planting, it's become an annual spring tradition to grab a few of my bedding plants and make a centerpiece to serve with my coffee and croissants. Along with violas, pansies and sweet alyssum are also good plants as candidates to use this way, just to name a few.

Opposite: Public gardens planted in large displays of colorful annual bedding plants such as these violas were quite popular in the Victorian age. The well-to-do believed that gardens would improve the manners of the lower class and quiet social unrest. A passion for collecting exotic plants throughout the British Empire spurred the popularity of gardens planted in intricate patterns and designs. It seems fitting that we should use these colorful annuals to enjoy indoors as well.

collections | CREAMWARE AND ITS KIN

The story of how I came to collect ceramic dishes begins with an ugly cupboard.

When I purchased my house, little of the original kitchen was left intact and the space was small with few remarkable features remaining except for a bank of windows and a rather humble-looking built-in cupboard with glass doors. The cabinet was painted the most putrid color of yellow you might imagine and the original hardware was long gone. What remained was sadly adorned with some faux brass Colonial knobs from the 1970s. As I renovated the kitchen, I added a black-and-white floor and decided to repaint the woodwork. Rather than draw attention to the cupboard, I decided to replace the old knobs with simple white ceramic handles that were affordable and stylish—perfect for an overbudget restoration! Those little ceramic knobs led me to start piling all of my white dishes into the cabinet. At first this was just an attempt to organize things. Then, along the way, it becáme a destination for a heap of white discordant objects (odds and ends that were mostly given to me by my family when I first set up housekeeping). The white ceramic items I have consist of both sublime and ridiculous objects that span the course of time from the eighteenth century to some of my latest purchases from the Pottery Barn, eBay, and the flea market. Most items that aren't plates and cups are practical in some way—mainly purchased with the idea of using them to display something from the garden—while others might be kindly described as useless curiosities. They make great table accents and often evoke conversations among friends and guests that begin something like this: "Where did you get that?" I find my favorites are the most bizarre and the least-paid-for objects. But the thing I like most about the collection is its color. White is white, and it goes with most anything and any style— from traditional to contemporary patterns—and all shapes and sizes commune effortlessly.

CITRUS FROM SEED

You can grow citrus trees from a seed, but because of the length of time it takes the plant to mature and the chance that it will not produce fruit, you'll get better results from buying the trees.

20. Keep Fruits at Your Fingertips

Gardeners delight in growing the perfect tomato or even a few herbs for cooking. But when it comes to citrus fruits, most of us depend on someone else to supply that kind of produce. So it may come as a surprise that there are several varieties of dwarf citrus trees that make growing lemons, Key limes, Calamondin oranges, and kumquats as simple as caring for a houseplant. Their fresh fruit, fragrant blooms, and glossy green leaves are a joy to have indoors during the winter or close at hand on the patio during warm weather. I grow an 'Improved Meyer' lemon tree and look forward to moving it inside when it is in flower.

Meyer lemons are a cross between a lemon and an orange, which accounts for their sublime flavor. My tree supplies me with just enough lemons to make one of my favorite desserts, lemon chess pie, which always reminds me of the delicious finale to many a family meal.

The origin of the name chess pie is uncertain, but there are plenty of guesses and a bit of folklore surrounding the name. The story I like to tell is about the northerner who came south for a visit and asked the cook what she was baking that smelled so great. When she answered "Just pie" in her southern dialect, the northerner thought she said "chess pie," and so the name stuck.

Lemon Chess Pie   MAKES ONE 9-INCH PIE

1 9-inch pie crust (your recipe or refrigerated premade crust)	²⁄₃ cup light brown sugar
	½ teaspoon salt
	1 tablespoon lemon zest
5 large egg yolks	2 tablespoons lemon juice
1 large egg	½ stick butter
1 cup buttermilk	Whipped cream and
²⁄₃ cup sugar	lemon rind for garnish

1. Preheat the oven to 350°F. Place the pie crust into a 9-inch pie pan.
2. In a large mixing bowl, beat together the egg yolks, egg, buttermilk, sugars, salt, lemon zest, and lemon juice. Cut the butter into the mixture and melt it by setting the bowl over a larger container of boiling water. Stir until the butter melts completely.
3. Pour the mixture into the crust and bake for 70 minutes until all but the center is firm—it will firm up once the pie cools.
4. Serve with whipped cream and lemon rind, if desired.

Opposite: The fragrance from my 'Improved Meyer' lemon tree blooms is like nectar from the gods, and it is delightful to watch the fruit develop.

21. Create a Tabletop Garden

Clustering baskets of spring blooms near a doorstep creates an inviting welcome for a special event, but once the party is over the flowers often don't get the attention they deserve. After the foot traffic slows down, bring the arrangement indoors and display the plants on a tabletop where you can enjoy their fragrance and beauty at eye level. This collection of tulips, hyacinths, muscari or grape hyacinths, and violas can be packed together, left in their plastic nursery pots, and concealed in moss-covered wire baskets. Or you can pop them out of their containers and plant them as a group. If you use a wire basket, as I did, protect your furniture by lining the inside of the moss with a plastic bag. That way, when you water your plants and the pots drain, the water won't spill out and spot your table.

Look for spring flowers in grocery stores and garden centers. If you are buying the plants a week or so before the event, choose plants that are still in bud and just beginning to show color so you can enjoy them longer, but if you are buying them the day of the party, you'll probably want them in full bloom. To prolong their colorful show, put them on view in a cool spot out of direct sun and keep them watered.

Opposite: Once spring-flowering bulbs are enjoyed indoors, you may want to plant them outside to bloom again next year. That works for some bulbs better than others. Daffodils, muscari, and crocus generally do well replanted in the garden. As soon as the ground is workable in the spring, gently lift the bulbs out of their pots, taking care not to damage the roots, and plant them in the garden. Give them water and some slow-release bulb food. Then wait until the leaves turn brown and die back naturally. Tulips and hyacinths are less reliable and may come back, but not with the same full, robust blooms.

grow your own

Enjoy spring on your timetable by forcing bulbs into bloom at home. Tulips, daffodils, hyacinths, and crocuses can be planted in containers in late summer or early fall.

Select containers that have drainage holes and partially fill them with potting soil.

Set the bulbs so that the tops are slightly below the rim of the container.

Add more potting soil until the tops stick out and then water each container thoroughly.

Keep the containers in cold storage (35–45°F) for 12 to 16 weeks. Consider using a spare refrigerator, unheated garage, root cellar, or a cold frame.

Remove the containers of potted bulbs from cold storage and put them in a cool (50–60°F), semidark location.

After several days, move the plants to a slightly warmer area that receives bright light and keep the soil evenly moist.

Flowering should occur in 3 to 4 weeks.

For a succession of blooms, remove pots from cold storage at 10- to 14-day intervals.

22. Pick the Right Houseplant

Houseplants add such a lively element to our homes that it's great to use them as accents in any area that needs a little lift. Most houseplants are tropical plants that are able to adapt to our home environments. But as anyone who has grown houseplants knows, some are a bit fussier than others. If you're like me, you don't have time to do much more than occasionally water a plant. If it needs special care, the plant doesn't last very long. So through trial and error, I've found there are some that are better suited to my style of living.

In areas such as the kitchen I can use plants that enjoy a little more humidity and bright indirect light. One of my favorites, and a fun choice for children, is the white rabbit's-foot fern (*Humata tyermannii*). This plant has silvery white fuzzy "feet" (stems or rhizomes) that creep outside of whatever container it's grown in.

Another good choice for low-light areas in your kitchen is the Chinese evergreen (*Aglaonema*). It has been a well-loved houseplant since it was first brought to the United States from the Southeast Asia rain-forest in 1900. The foliage has beautiful cream-colored streaks that brighten any darkened corner.

In the Resource Guide (page 213), you'll find a list of other easy-care houseplants.

Left: Rabbit's-foot fern enjoys bright indirect light, so avoid placing it in a window with direct southern sun. When the temperature is comfortable for you, that's just right for this plant. Since more ferns are harmed by overwatering than holding back on the water, it's best to water the fern well and then allow it to dry lightly before watering again. When mature the plant will develop brown circles under the leaves. These are not bugs, they are spores. They aren't harmful. Spores are to ferns what seeds are to other plants. **Opposite:** Real life becomes a reflection of the painting. It's almost as if the potted red geranium on the blue-striped cloth served as a model for the still-life painting.

23. Mix Art and Flowers

Coming from a family of amateur artists and enjoying the activity myself, original works of art often catch my eye as I prowl through the dusty back rooms of antiques stores and flea markets. I guess part of me hopes I'll stumble across some overlooked masterpiece being sold for next to nothing by someone with an unschooled eye. This idea probably came from watching one too many episodes of *Antiques Roadshow* on public television.

When I find paintings that I like, I'm often tempted to buy many more than I have wall space to display them, so to help me narrow my focus and limit my appetite, I decided to set a price limit of one hundred dollars for those I purchase. It has been a delightful surprise to discover that there are all kinds of wonderful bargains in that price range.

When I bring a painting home, I clean it off and prop it up on my counter so I can admire it. The picture often seems lonely and forlorn, so I like to find a plant to place near it that picks up the colors in the painting. Much like when I'm designing a garden, I like to use the colors, shapes, and styles of elements in the setting as springboards for my plant choices. So if I want to build on a picture's bold colors and high energy, I'll look for contrasting hues and shapes in the plants to add vibrancy to the mix. Colors that are on the opposite sides of the color wheel offer the most contrast, such as yellow and purple, red and green, blue and orange. But if I want plants that gently blend with the art, I'll use similar hues and repeating shapes to create a soothing mix.

This is my simplified version of a popular event held at many art museums around the country called "Art in Bloom." There you can see the likes of Picasso, Klee, and de Kooning with interpretive flower arrangements juxtaposed with their works. The ticketed event always draws a huge crowd of admirers. While I won't be selling tickets for my creations, it's a fun and easy way to mix art and plants, and something that works in any decor.

collections / NAÏVE PICTURES

I grew up in a family of dabblers. It seems at one time or another someone in my family tried every conceivable arts-and-crafts project, be it ceramics, decoupage, scrapbooking, jewelry making, even macramé. So, as you can imagine, painting was also a part of our embracement of the arts, and as a result there were countless naïve, often terribly bad paintings produced by someone in my family. These painting binges came in waves, and when the call to paint was heard, paint they did. The subjects in the pictures usually consisted of bowls of fruit, the occasional landscape, or a pet, and when one ventured near portraiture the results were usually tragic.

One cousin, however, broke out of the pack and became an exceptional artist. With that, the idea that the family had some artistic talent and harbored the genes of great painters became part of our family's lore. However, what I saw as evidence of most of my relatives' talents clearly proved otherwise. Still, several paintings possessed a sweet naïve character rendered by the hand of dilettantes, and this endearing quality has remained with me. So when I'm in antiques stores, junk shops, and flea markets, I find pleasure in stumbling onto simple little pictures, many from the late nineteenth century, but most from the early 1900s, that remind me of my family's paintings. I never spend more than a hundred dollars on one of these gems, and many I find for much less than that!

24. *Capture Seasonal Splendors*

In a world where strawberries and roses are available year-round, the uniqueness of their arrival in our gardens is somewhat diminished. That's why I like to celebrate the abundance of garden delights when they are in season. However, I often forget to gather them and bring them into the house. How many times have I walked past my wisteria in spring and never cut some of the plants' glorious blooms? The brief time the lavender racemes drape the garden in their sweet fragrance is the time to gather as much of its beauty and hold it for as long as possible. When I'm ready to arrange them in the house, because the blooms are so generous and full, I often display the cuttings alongside a piece of heavy statuary. The visual weight of both seems to be a good pairing. While you may not have wisteria blooming in your garden, put yourself in tune with the seasonal offerings in the landscape, be they flowers or fruit, and gather some to bring inside. I found the sideboard in my kitchen to be a beautiful spot for this arrangement, but it could be placed anywhere you want to be reminded of a season's special offering.

Opposite: There are two regular types of wisterias available, the Japanese (*W. floribunda*) and the Chinese (*W. sinensis*). In the garden, both are vigorous growers and need strong support or heavy pruning to keep them from taking over. Plant your vine near a very sturdy trellis or arbor. You can also train them to grow as small trees or standards.

WISTERIA WON'T BLOOM?

If your wisteria doesn't flower, find out if it was grown from seed. It takes 10 to 15 years for a seed-grown plant to bloom. When purchasing a wisteria plant, make sure it was propagated by grafting or cutting. Plant it in full sun, and fertilize only once a year.

25. *Use Garden Center Finds*

It's easy to overlook nurseries as places to shop for plants to use inside the house. But even if your yard is so small there's no place to sink a shovel, your local garden center offers a wealth of beautiful plants for your home. It's understandable why many people drive right by a garden center when they are out shopping for flowers for a dining-room centerpiece. The notion is supported by the way these stores are often organized. Most nurseries divide their plants into separate departments, such as annuals, trees, shrubs, and perennials. If they do sell houseplants, they are often far in the back by themselves.

I say, why not mix it up? Peruse the aisle of your local garden center looking for plants that catch your eye. Consider bringing shrubs and perennials into your kitchen or dining area. They come in all sizes, and when they are in full bloom they make handsome additions to your home's interior landscape. If the plant has a great look and it complements the color and scale of your interior, give it a try.

Now, there are certain caveats to follow, and shelf life is one of them. Most of these plants make great houseguests for about a week to ten days, after which it's time to move them back outside. But that's when you'll benefit from the double-duty quality of this technique. Enjoy them inside and then plant them outside—either in your flower bed or, if space is limited, in containers by your door. Just keep in mind when you are selecting a plant to use indoors that it will do best displayed in a location with light conditions similar to those it needs outside. Just check the plant tag for that information. Have fun with the idea and display your nursery finds in imaginative containers combined with other interior accents.

Left: As the hellebore's blossoms mature, they take on a soft green cast.
Opposite: The combination of these two early-blooming nursery plants, a shrub called Ogon spirea and a perennial called 'HGC Green Corsican' helleborus, brings out the best in each. The spirea's small white five-petaled blossoms contrast nicely with the hellebore's compact mounded form and flowers.

Glassware in various shapes and sizes is the "little black dress" of the flower-arranging world. It goes with any decor and can be dressed up or down with the choice of plants and objects around it. You can never have too much of this stuff. I collect glassware in every shape, size, and style imaginable. Whether it's big apothecary jars for terrariums, antique water bottles for long-stemmed flowers, juice glasses for mini-bouquets, or cut-glass champagne flutes for sipping port, I find them useful in a multitude of ways. And one of the beauties of collecting glassware is you can find it everywhere—from junk shops to estate sales—in all price ranges. When I find a style I like, I often buy more than one of a kind because they work well used as multiple containers throughout a room or lined up to create a parade of flowers.

The clarity of glass allows you to see the entire plants and all of their parts, which can sometimes be more interesting than the most seductive of blooms. In spring I often gently lift bulbs and rinse the soil from their roots and display them in clear glass containers. If you try this, remember that it will take multiple rinsings in cold tap water to get the roots clean enough so the water in the glass remains clear and pristine. Also, do not add anything else to the water to enhance the plant's longevity; clear water is best.

26. Show Off a Plant's Stems

When it comes to displaying plants inside, stems simply don't get their due. Sure, some florist materials are grown strictly for their stems, such as plants like the yellow- or red-twig dogwoods and the coral-bark Japanese maple 'Sangu Kaku'. But, I must stand up for the stems of the plants we cut from our gardens. Tall vertical bundles of stalks viewed through clear glass have their own appeal. The blooms are often just the icing on the cake. Tall glass bottles make this approach a stylish effect that can be created quickly with little fuss.

WATER-RING REMOVAL

To remove a water ring in a glass flower vase, fill the vase with a 50-50 solution of water and white vinegar and let it soak overnight.

The long-stemmed snowflakes (*Leucojum aestivum*) that bloom in my garden often flower about the time of my earliest spring daffodils. They grow from bulbs and each stalk produces two to five small (1 inch) delicate white flowers that hang in a graceful arc. Each petal on the snow white blossom has a small emerald spot near its tip. Snowflakes are perennials that will spread and create a beautiful mass of flowers and foliage.

One spring as I gathered them from my garden, I noticed how the flowers were held aloft on long beautiful stalks that were hidden in the bed of foliage. I began to think about what I had that could show off their long stately stems. As I began rummaging around in the dining room, my eye caught my collection of narrow-neck water bottles. Their shape and size were perfect for putting small handfuls of flowers in each vase.

Above: Summer snowflakes are one of the easiest and most carefree naturalizing bulbs you can grow. They thrive in full sun to light shade or under shrubs and trees that are leafless in late winter and early spring. The bulbs do best in soil that is moist but well drained, especially when they are in flower. After they bloom, be sure to leave the vegetation alone so it can recharge the bulb. After a few weeks it will die back naturally. Once the plant is dormant in summer, it can tolerate drought. Summer snowflakes grow in Zones 4–9. In the warmest parts of the country the flower blooms in late autumn and winter, but elsewhere it flowers in very early spring. **Opposite:** Because the blooms of the snowflake flowers are so dainty, I wanted to display them in something, such as these cut-glass bottles, that wouldn't compete with their charm.

PLANT COLLECTIONS

Nursery Finds

There are few things in life I look forward to more than my first visit to the nursery in spring. It is such a rush to see what new plants can be found and to revisit my old favorites. The sheer variety of all the annuals, perennials, shrubs, trees, and vines that are available is amazing. When I operated a garden center with my family, May was our busiest month, with gardeners crowding the aisles in search of special treasures. It was a rare shopper who purchased the plants with the idea of using them as interior accents. On your next visit to a garden center, see what you can find.

1. *Japanese maple* (Acer palmatum *var.* dissectum)

2. *Camellia* (Camellia sasanqua *'Maiden's Blush'*)

3. *Forsythia* (Forsythia x intermedia)

4. *Clematis* (Clematis *hybrid 'Marie Louise Jensen'*)

5. *Pineapple lily* (Eucomis *spp.*)

6. *Ornamental peppers* (Capsicum annuum *'Chilly Chili'*)

7. *Osteospermum daisies* (Osteospermum *hybrid 'Lemon Symphony'*)

8. *American beautyberry* (Callicarpa americana)

9. *Sweetspire* (Itea virginica *'Little Henry'*)

If you love history, particularly anything that is garden related, old prints can become an obsession. Every antiques mall or antiques show has at least one vendor who specializes in prints. The craze for this artwork has probably done more to contribute to the destruction of books and folios from libraries (collections) than any other single force or act.

I bought my first two copper-plate engravings from a rare-book seller (Lloyd's of Kew) in London in 1985. They are views of Richard Chambers's Antique Arch built in Kew Gardens and first printed in 1782. Prior to photography, copper-plate engraving was the primary method of producing images on paper for printmaking and illustrations in books and magazines. An intaglio printing plate made of copper was created by incising the surface with the design, covering the plate in thick ink, and wiping it to leave the ink in the incisions. A damp piece of paper was placed on top of the plate and then the plate and paper were run through a printing press that, through pressure, transferred the ink from the recesses of the plate to the paper. When I learned about the many steps to this process, it gave me a better appreciation for the beauty and intricacies of the designs that were created in this way. The engravings became a curiosity to me in part because these images represented the way a reader came to learn about unknown places or to see how exotic animals and plants might appear.

Some of the illustrations in my collection range from detailed and lifelike images to those that appear exaggerated and cartoonlike. I have pictures of various breeds of chickens, Native Americans, reptiles, domestic animals, and British and American worthies, but the ones that bring me the most pleasure are landscape plans from the eighteenth and nineteenth centuries. As the copyrights of many of these have long expired, they are available to be duplicated and used in novel ways. I've reproduced them as placemats, wrapping paper, table decorations, and lampshades. These old garden prints make bringing the garden to the table whimsical and fun.

27. Set a Scene

The art of dining in the home doesn't seem as practiced these days as it was years ago. I'm guilty of it myself. It's easy to fall into the trap of feeling there is not enough time to make dinner as well as put out my best dishes. But don't you love to go to a dinner party where the host has applied some creativity to the table setting or laid a theme in place for the evening?

I've found one way to ensure that I'll take the time to sit down and enjoy a meal in my dining room is to either host a dinner party or put a date on the calendar when I schedule enough time to treat myself and a few close friends to a special time together. When the day arrives, it becomes a welcome break in the routine and reconnects me to my home and the bounty of the garden.

To make the evening special, I draw inspiration from my collections; if I don't have something I need, I will borrow objects and equally share what I have. For instance, I've taken some of my old engraved prints of seventeenth-century French garden plans and copied them in a color copier to make placemats and used my antique flower frogs as delightful card placeholders. Everything doesn't have to be the same; mixing and matching dishes creates a fun blend of styles.

Left: Branches from a fig tree add a touch of greenery to the table setting. Several clear glass bottles are arranged down the center of the table, creating an elevated centerpiece that doesn't interfere with the flow of the conversation. Condition the tree branches by cutting them early in the morning and placing them in a bucket of water in a cool dark place until you are ready to use them. **Opposite:** While grand displays have their place, simple and bold can be equally effective. Along with fig tree branches, other interesting plants that could be used in this way include palm, ruscus, leucothe, fern fronds, birds of paradise, and hostas.

28. Try Vegetables in Place of Flowers

On the spur of the moment, after a late-summer afternoon in the garden harvesting an assortment of squash and gourds, I decided to invite some friends over for dinner. With no time to cut flowers for a centerpiece, I spied my just-picked basket of vegetables and decided to pile them on a plate for a quick arrangement. I was so pleased with the results that I've since created several variations of the idea, combining different varieties of squash and gourds.

Through trial and error, I found these arrangements looked best displayed on an elevated cake plate so the forms are lifted off the table. It also helps to add a touch of foliage to break up the mass of fruits or vegetables. This approach can be particularly effective in late summer and early fall when themes of abundance and plenitude fit the spirit of the season. And if you don't have a garden, these vegetables are easily found in grocery stores or farmers' markets. Look for vegetables in three sizes—large, medium, and small—and in colors that are compatible together and will harmonize with your table setting.

SQUASH TERMS

Squash are loosely categorized as either summer and winter varieties. Summer squash (zucchinis, yellow crooked neck) are thin-skinned, and keep for just a short time, requiring little to no cooking. Winter squash (pumpkins, acorn, butternut) keep for months without refrigeration, and must be cooked to soften their thick skins.

Opposite: The colorful skins of these winter squash—'Delicata', 'Hi Beta Gold' spaghetti squash, 'Table King' acorn squash, and 'Golden Hubbard' squash—are accented with clusters of wild pears and cut tips from tree branches that have tiny acorns.

29. *Elevate the Centerpiece*

I have to watch myself when I'm putting together a centerpiece. I can get so drawn in to creating the art and the movement in the arrangement that I forget about the purpose, effect, and most important, the guests! As anyone who has tried to talk to someone on the other side of the dinner table knows, a centerpiece can easily become a distraction if not kept to a scale that allows you to see the other person. While we often think that translates to a centerpiece with a low profile, another option is to elevate the display above eye level. A special piece in my silver collection helps me do just that.

LIGHTING VOTIVES

Lighting lots of votives and candles before guests arrive can be a chore, and if you're like me you always burn your fingertips while trying to get the match to meet the wick in those tiny jars. Try using a piece of dried spaghetti. It works great if you light it with a match first.

Throughout the year, I enjoy using my early-19th-century Irish silver epergne in my dining room to hold things gathered from my garden. The bowl just invites bounty without overpowering the setting. Here I've filled it with wild and domesticated pears. On other occasions it has held nandina berries and apples, an assortment of gourds, and a collection of orchids. The small votives encircling the base create a warm glow that dances off the silver. Surrounding the epergne are several clipped boxwoods planted in silver mint julep cups creating the feel of a French parterre garden.

Opposite and overleaf: For special occasions, it's fun to pull out all the stops and set an elegant table. The crowning glory is golden-skinned wild and Bosc pears piled high in my silver epergne that is encircled with votives and mini-boxwoods. The round globes of the boxwoods echo the forms of other circular shapes around the table, while offering some color and textural contrast.

The passion to accumulate these dishes started like so many of my collections, with a single piece. I was browsing through a shop when my eyes fell on a small gravy boat. It was easy to imagine it filled with something from the garden, so my gaze lingered. I found its simple gold-and-white pattern quite appealing. As I was admiring the piece, a friend who knew I also collected Paris porcelain floral vases pointed out that these dishes were also made during that same period. That's all I needed to hear. I was hooked and started looking for more pieces every time I popped into an antiques shop or flea market. And so my collection grew.

Some of the dishes in my collection are in great shape, while others show their age with chips and cracks and places where the gold banding has worn away. Do I care? No matter what its condition, anytime I'm on the hunt for another piece and find one, I bag it and bring it home. The serving dishes are the most useful for flowers, from the smallest salt cellar to the commodious soup tureen, and they are close at hand so I can pull them off the shelf and use them in displays. And like antique silver, this old porcelain sets an engaging table because all the pieces are slightly different, a quality that adds to the charm of dining with them.

As a kid I remember seeing these sets (many complete) in antebellum houses in the Mississippi River delta area. They were ordered by planters and delivered from France to the port of New Orleans and then distributed to households in the region. My collection represents the fragments of those sets that graced the tables in dining rooms of many of those homes over a span of 175 years.

30. Revisit a Classic

Being an avowed "roseaholic," my mission is to convince as many people as possible that growing roses is a joy and a luxury not to be missed. Sadly, roses have the undeserved reputation of being fussy and difficult to maintain. But as those who are willing to give it a try have discovered, they are worth the effort and bring immense pleasure.

The roses I particularly enjoy growing are the old-fashioned varieties. These are the plants that were developed before 1876. Many have intriguing histories, such as the rose 'Souvenir de la Malmaison', originally known as 'Queen of Beauty and Fragrance'. This rose received its present name when one of the grand dukes of Russia obtained a specimen for the Imperial Garden in St. Petersburg after visiting Malmaison, the gardens developed by Napoléon's first empress, Joséphine. It's fun and fascinating to be able to look at the flower in my garden and know I am admiring such heritage. It was Joséphine who was the first to import and distribute many of the species that are so familiar to us today—gathering together plants from captured ships sailing between the New and Old Worlds and bringing others from her native Martinique to her home in Rueil-Malmaison, just outside Paris. From there, she generously sent cuttings to her friends as well as to rulers of countries, so eventually the plants spread to enthusiasts in surprisingly far-flung places.

Not only do I find the history of these heritage roses fascinating, I also find them to be more carefree and adaptable than their hybrid tea cousins. If you are interested in exploring these varieties, look for roses labeled "heritage," "old garden," or "old-fashioned" at your local garden center or through a mail-order source. If you have ever shopped for a rose, you know that there are hundreds to choose from. To help make the selection easier, I've listed several of my favorites according to site-specific or characteristic-specific categories; see "A Rose for Every Garden" in the Resource Guide, page 210. Many of these are true old-fashioned, but I've also slipped in a few modern varieties.

Roses make a spectacular statement when planted in any garden. They are so versatile that they can be used in several ways. Since many of the climbers are vigorous growers, they add a romantic touch to an arched entry into the garden. I also like to create a rustic teepee from three tree limbs and let the roses twine around the poles. And if you're looking for a colorful alternative to a hedge, many of these beauties are ideal when planted in a row. In my garden I enjoy them as flowering shrubs, integrating them among perennials and annuals to create a beautiful mixed border.

Not only are roses a joy in the garden, but they are also a pleasure in the house. There are few things better than cutting an armload of blossoms for arrangements to adorn the dining room. When roses are displayed in silver pieces it will take your breath away! The two beauties just seem to be meant for each other.

Opposite: No place or time to grow your own roses? You can still enjoy their fragrance and beauty by purchasing a bouquet to create an arrangement like this. Fresh-cut roses are now readily found in grocery stores and are often combined with other plants such as stock, freesia, and eucalyptus. Starting with a purchased bouquet, I just added some foliage cut from the garden, including evergreen stems of arborvitae and the silvery leafed 'Flashy Lady' dusty miller to create this arrangement.

collections | OLD SILVER

A few years ago, during a photo shoot in my home, the editor of a popular home magazine told me that all my dining-room silver would need to be removed. You can only imagine my reaction. I had anticipated that I might have to cut it back a bit or have it restyled or rearranged—but removed? She said it was "too fancy." My reply was, "Not this stuff!" Just because it's silver doesn't mean it's expensive. Many of my favorite pieces I've picked up for a song.

Like so many of my collections, the silver I have springs from a love of beautiful things that are useful, and there's no doubt I put mine to work. As far as displaying silver, I like having it on the tops of sideboards, chests, and the silent butler in the dining room. It is a compendium of bits and bobs, some left with a sparkle, some plated pieces that are well worn down to the copper or brass base. Rarely is it polished (apart from the cutlery and pieces used for meals or events). But there is nothing like candlelight and lots of old silver to transform a dining room into a magical space.

31. Try a Squeeze Play

If a plant will not fit into a particular container because the container size or root-ball is too large, don't worry. I've found that by gently washing the soil away from the roots you can reduce the soil mass so the plant will fit in a small container. Plants are more forgiving than you might think. By taking this approach you can reduce their size by 50 percent or more. Just keep the roots moist. This will allow you to put the most extraordinary nursery plants in the teenie-weeniest containers such as these boxwoods in mint julep cups. Surprisingly, many of these plants have a high-survival rate if not left indoors too long in their constricted state, say a week or so, and then moved outside into more commodious conditions. If the idea of reducing the roots this much makes you nervous, avoid trying it on your most precious or expensive plants.

cleaning silver

To polish your silver, try this quick tarnish remover. Wash the pieces and place them on a sheet of aluminum foil in the bottom of a 2-quart pot. In another pot in the sink, mix together a solution of ¼ cup baking soda to a quart of boiling water. Carefully pour that mixture over the silver and let it stand for a few minutes. Remove the silver and rinse. Repeat if necessary.

Above: After the boxwoods had their debut at a formal dinner party, I wanted to enjoy them a few more days, so I moved them into the kitchen and put them on a plate stand to give them their own starring role. If you use containers such as these mint julep cups, which don't have drainage holes, it is important not to overwater the plants.

32. Float Some Blooms

Anyone who has ever seen Monet's water lilies gets this idea. There is something so mesmerizing and sensual about blooms floating in water. This is the easiest flower arrangement you'll ever create! Simply pick the flowers, trim the stems short, add water to a wide-mouth bowl, and place the blooms on the surface. You'll find some flowers are better suited for this than others. The trick is to select fresh blossoms that have a large surface area. Camellias, chrysanthemums, marigolds, cosmos, and daisies make good floating flowers. Many of these are ones I have in my garden because they are so easy to grow. My camellia shrubs bloom in late winter or early spring so their flowers are always a welcome burst of color as a centerpiece. Floating the flowers allows me to really pack in the blossoms and make the most of their delightful fragrance and beauty.

My trifle bowl has been used many more times as a container for flowers than for serving dessert. By looking at your dishes as potential flower holders, you may discover lots of new ways to use things you have in your cupboard. Let the flowers guide your choice of container. The camellias have the look and feel of a party and are best displayed in a glass bowl so nothing competes with the bloom. Marigolds and chrysanthemums have a more informal feel, so using a blue ceramic bowl with rustic accessories complements the flowers.

Below: After a few days you may find that the outer petals of some of your floating flowers are turning brown. To renew your display, simply remove the flowers, fill the bowl with fresh water, and gently pull off the browning petals. **Opposite:** Successfully mixing flowers and fabric can be tricky. One rule of thumb to follow is to use a bold design, such as this striped material, and large blooms. They tend to balance each other rather than one dominating the display.

33. Redefine Garden Containers

They say necessity is the mother of invention, and that was the case when I was setting things out for a buffet at my house. I ran out of space on the sideboard to put out my silverware. The terra-cotta urns were sitting idly by so I decided it was time to put them to work. Now they are a regular accessory to my serving table. I simply fill them with rice to serve as an anchor and tuck the silverware inside.

USE FILLERS

When planting oversized garden containers, fill the majority of the volume with something inert and lightweight, such as Bubble Wrap, Styrofoam, or a large garbage bag full of empty black plastic nursery pots (this is a great way to reuse the pots). Then cover the filler with potting soil and plants. Most annuals, perennials, houseplants, and many shrubs only need 10–12 inches of soil to thrive.

On another occasion, a friend who was moving didn't want to haul his large cast-iron urn to his next home and sold it to me for a song. There was no place for it in the garden, so it sat empty for a year in storage. One winter, when I was rearranging my dining room, I wanted something tall in the corner and remembered the urn. It needed a little extra height, so I placed it on top of a column and planted it with the striking form of a large agave. It was the perfect accent piece.

When you begin to view the world as inside out and vice versa, you see how playful decorating a garden home can become. Look for opportunities to bring your garden ornaments and vessels into the house and put them to use.

Left: The baked-clay look of terra-cotta objects, whether they are as simple as a standard clay pot or as ornate as these urns and bust, give interior spaces an instant garden-like quality. **Opposite:** This scenic panel called *Monuments of Paris* is a hand-blocked print by Zuber et Cie, a French wallpaper manufacturer popular in this country from the 1820s to 1840s. The large iron urn in front of the screen helps give the scene some added dimension.

Twin Topiaries

I love rummaging around the woods for flora to gather for autumn displays. It is amazing what you can find if you keep your eyes and mind open. On one foray I collected an assortment of leaves, flowers, seedpods, and berries and decided to create matching topiaries for the sideboard in my dining room.

2 matching urns

2 plastic dishes to protect urns

2 soaked floral foam cones or bricks (see page 29),
   plus extra bricks for height

Knife

Floral tape

Floral picks

Lazy Susan (optional)

Fall leaves, wild pears, chrysanthemums, dahlias,
   okra, china, ligustrum, Chinese photinia and
   callicarpa berries, bittersweet vines, and rosehips

Pruners

Floral pins

1. If the urn isn't waterproof, place a plastic dish inside to hold floral foam. Insert soaked floral foam in the urn and cut it with a knife so it is wedged into the urn and sits flush with the top.

2. Tape the foam to the urn. Insert floral picks in the bottom foam and push the top cone onto the picks to hold the two pieces of foam together. If available, set the urn on a lazy Susan so the arrangement can be easily turned while it is being assembled.

3. Trim the ends of the plant material with pruners to the desired length. Begin at the base of the cone and insert foliage. Work around and up, inserting the larger elements, such as the flowers, fruit, and seed clusters, into the foam, distributing them evenly, and then fill in with smaller flowers, leaves, and berries. Use floral pins as needed. Small sections of vines can be added last.

Done!

34. Grow Windowsill Herbs

Garden topiaries are a wonderful art form in which evergreen plants with small leaves and a dense form, such as boxwood (*Buxus sempervirens*), holly (*Ilex* spp.), or privet (*Ligustrum* spp.) are clipped into sculptures. Sometimes the plant is shaped into a geometric form and other times the shape is something more fanciful like a life-sized elephant. Gardeners have been pruning plants into topiaries for some two thousand years. There are wonderful examples of garden topiary all over the world. The Ladew Topiary Gardens just north of Baltimore, Maryland, has some outstanding examples. Its best-known topiary depicts a fox hunt with horses, riders, dogs, and a fox all clearing a hedge.

Above: Herbs need at least five hours of sun each day. A south or southeast window is ideal. Water sparingly and only use fertilizers and pest controls labeled for use on edibles.

You can keep a part of this age-old tradition alive by adding topiaries to your home. They blend well with almost any decor because they are part plant and part sculpture with pleasing geometric shapes that are classic and timeless. You can find "premade" topiaries in garden centers or florist shops where houseplants are sold that are clipped and shaped into various forms, so all you need to do is maintain them. Or if you'd prefer to grow them yourself, you can either buy a form (online or in craft stores) and train vining plants such as ivy to grow on the form and take on the shape, or you can purchase plants that can be pruned into the form you'd like.

My favorite topiaries are those made from herbs, because they are both beautiful and useful. Every time I clip the branches to keep them shaped up, I add the aromatic leaves to a recipe or create a fragrant bouquet. Stop by a garden center, and you'll see a wide variety of herbs in all different shapes and sizes. Some of the best herbs for topiaries include rosemary, lavender, trailing thyme, myrtle, and santolina.

collections | TERRA-COTTA

The phrase *terra-cotta* literally means "baked earth." Most recognize it as unglazed porous clayware formed into objects like flower pots. Some terra-cotta samples found along the Nile River have dated to around 10,000 BC, making it one of the oldest home and garden accessories. Today, you can find containers made from terra-cotta in a subtle range of colors, as well as various degrees of porosity and cold tolerance—all factors that influence its quality. It's always disappointing to find a favorite clay pot broken and unusable after being left outside in the cold, but there are some terra-cotta containers that can hold up in subzero temperatures. Some of the best clay comes from the hillsides of Impruneta, Italy. Its mineral content gives it a high frost tolerance that allows containers made from the clay to withstand temperatures as low as 20 degrees F without cracking. The clay that gives it its strength also produces a color that is softer and more pastel than the bright orange clay typically seen. Although it is more expensive, it has durability that is unmatched and it is gentler on the eye when placed in the garden because of its mellow color.

I find the classically shaped terra-cotta container to be an easy fit in almost any garden style and can be seamlessly integrated inside the home to hold houseplants as well. The material can be used for much more than a stack of clay pots in the garage. One of my favorite pieces is a sculpture of a woman's head I found in a shop in a side street in Florence. It is a terra-cotta copy of Canova's *Helen of Troy*. I literally cradled her in my lap all the way home on the airplane for fear she would be damaged if I shipped her.

One of the most versatile rooms in the house is the living room. Today it comes in many sizes and is called different things, depending on its use. It can be your family's favorite hangout or a guests-only "parlor," or it can serve as a music room, library, TV room, or den. Once you script the room's role, selecting embellishments to set the mood is a matter of your taste and style.

Above all it should reflect your individuality. The key to exhibiting your interest in gardening inside your home is to use your imagination and see an item for not just what it is right now, but what it can be. Begin to envision objects displayed in new ways. When I moved a large cast-iron container from the back of my shed to the middle of a table in my den, it was suddenly transformed into a completely new object. And once I filled it with cut branches from my maple

Living
Room

tree adorned with spring colors, it became as unique and captivating as an original work of art.

In my home, a more formal living room opens onto an area that I use to relax, listen to music, and read. Both rooms are filled with a mix of my collections and garden-inspired accents. Over the years I've gathered a hodgepodge of odds and ends of furniture and decorative items that have acquired a sense of coherence. I enjoy that quality in a living room. My inspiration for this approach to decorating was my garden. When I first began I used plants, paths, and structures to define the basic structure of each area, and then I added combinations of plants to fill out the framework to further define its style. To be sure, these items were carefully placed, but I also left room for plants that would grow, spread, self-seed, and pop up wherever they wanted to take root, resulting in a mix that looks natural and organized. Inside, I use that same method of establishing a framework of the living room with large pieces of furniture, flooring, and wall color and then allow other elements to evolve and fill in as I find them and rearrange displays in the room. Another way to bring the feeling of the outdoors into my living area is to select a wall color that matches the foliage of the needlepoint holly hedge that is visible through the windows of this room. It was fun to take a leaf to the paint store and ask the owner to find a match. Now as I sit in the room and look outside there is a continuity of colors that helps blend interior and exterior spaces.

The most important quality in both indoor and outdoor living spaces is a sense of relaxed comfort that invites you to sit down and connect. Garden-style decorating helps you achieve that level of comfort by bringing the fresh-air feeling of the outdoors into your home.

Opposite, clockwise from top left: A favorite reading chair is even more inviting framed by a blooming hydrangea and the fragrance of potted herbs. The bold leaves of the upright elephant ear (*Alocasia macrorrhiza*) are a good match for the sleek and graphic lines of the living room furnishings. 'Babywing Pink' begonia is the perfect size to display indoors, growing to about a foot in height and width, with beautiful pink- to rose-colored blooms; it is the more diminutive version of its larger cousin, the 'Dragon Wing' begonia. A grouping of large glass bottles, each holding a single stem from a tropical plant, creates a striking arrangement.

35. *Cut Budding Branches*

If you have established trees and shrubs in your garden, they can serve as a ready source of material for arrangements indoors. One of my favorite cut branches to use is from the maple tree in my front yard. In early spring the tree's flowers and emerging leaves are the most exquisite shade of maroon, the perfect complement to my den's decor.

For cut branches to perform indoors, enhancing their ability to take up water is essential. If you buy them from a florist, when you get them home recut the stems immediately and put them into water. The woody stems of trees and shrubs take up water less easily than do the soft stems of herbaceous plants. To help your cuttings take up water, you can increase the stem's surface area in contact with water. First make your cut on a sharp diagonal, which has the added benefit of preventing the stem end from resting flat on the bottom of your container and getting plugged. You also should split the bottom of the stem about 1 to 4 inches, depending on the length of the stem. Old floral guides may tell you to crush the stem ends with a hammer, but this method has been discredited in favor of splitting them. Particles released in the water from the crushed stems tend to cloud the water and promote bacterial growth. Besides splitting the stems, to help cut down on bacterial growth in the water, remove any foliage that would fall below the waterline in the container and add a tablespoon of bleach per gallon of water.

I like to use long branches to make a dramatic arrangement and have found that they are best displayed in a large, heavy container that can counterbalance the length of the limbs and serve as a secure anchor should someone walk by and brush a branch. A cast-iron container from the garden is one of my favorite vessels to use. Its scale and mass are perfect for this type of arrangement. The idea is easily modified to any size area by being selective about the number and length of the branches you cut. However, the effect is more dramatic with large bundles.

36. Combine Collections

One of the most gratifying aspects of having collections is finding fun and unusual ways to put them to use. One of my favorite displays lets me combine three of my collections: ogee mirrors, cut-glass champagne flutes, and the delicate blooms of some special tulips I grow.

From time to time I like to use mirrors in my garden designs. This is certainly not a new idea but one worth employing when I want to make a space appear larger or give an area added dimension. When a mirror is used indoors as a surface for an arrangement of flowers, by simple reflection, the number of blooms is doubled. My collection of nineteenth-century ogee mirrors is handy this way. Laid flat they look like brown trays, and the

silvery surface is the perfect host for replicating the delicate and ephemeral blooms of some of my more treasured flowers. I'm also crazy for little cut-glass champagne flutes that are elegant for sipping port after a meal or to serve Prosecco in before. The little nineteenth-century glasses in my collection are probably the best thing I have in the glassware department. They are the perfect match for displaying delicate blooms such as species tulips (*Tulipa clusiana*) 'Lady Jane', which have a rosy red exterior with ivory white petal margins. I'm fascinated by species tulips that are different from the hybrid tulips that we more often see in gardens. Originally from the Mediterranean, Asia Minor, and the Caucasus, they offer unusual blossoms in varying heights and dazzling colors. Known to perennialize better than most tulips, they are wonderful for rock gardens and make sweet clusters in flower beds and naturalized drifts. As a cut flower, they are best appreciated as single specimens or loosely grouped together, as their delicate blossoms do not lend themselves to being muscled into arrangements with other flowers.

To create your own variation of this idea, gather the main elements: a mirror with a flat back that will lie evenly on a table, several small vases, and your choice of cut flowers; to add a beautiful glow, use candle-lit votives scattered among the vases. Turn the lights down low and transform the mood of your living room.

Above: Delicate 'Lady Jane' species tulips bask in the sun. **Opposite:** Trays, much like picture frames on the wall, are handy ways to "frame" an arrangement on a tabletop, helping to bring a collection of items into focus. They also make transporting several small vases or glasses from room to room much easier. Be sure to extinguish any flames before moving the tray.

I've collected ogee mahogany-veneer framed mirrors for many years. They get their name from the architectural term that describes the distinctively shaped profile of the frames. My attraction to the mirrors stems from the fact that they were made during the same time period as my collection of American Empire furniture, in the early to mid-1800s. If you're a collector, you know that's how it works: one obsession leads to the next.

The first three mirrors I purchased were part of an estate sale and I must say, they weren't in the best condition. They had been knocked around and were covered with dust, but I couldn't pass them up for sixty dollars apiece. Once I got them home, a little warm water, Old English furniture polish, and some elbow grease brought them back to life. As with all collections, the price of these mirrors seems to rise and fall. You can still get them at a reasonable price, but you have to prowl around to find them. I've been shocked at the prices I've seen for them at some high-end shops. When I do come across one I like, I'll buy it for its frame, whether it has its mirror or not, as I also found a talented man in a local glass shop who can replace the mirror and dress it up so it looks aged. Part of the fun of collecting is discovering people who can help restore these old beauties.

Mirrors in a narrow hallway reflect available light to help brighten the corridor and make it appear larger. When hanging mirrors of different sizes in a stairwell, use larger ones at the top and group smaller mirrors near the bottom to balance the perspective.

37. Display a Flowering Shrub

At our family-owned garden center, we often received large shipments of flowering shrubs such as azaleas, quince, hydrangeas, and viburnum to stock our store. As they were loaded off the truck, we would pack them together to create a mass of blooms for an attention-getting display of color. I was always struck by the beauty of the plants in their seasonal prime and thought they would make wonderful accents inside the home. Rather than cut the branches and set back the shrub, I began bringing containerized plants inside to enjoy for a week or so during their peak of blooms. After I saw how one shrub could instantly transform a room, I was hooked.

As you shop in garden centers, you'll find that shrubs usually come in various sizes, so you can pick the size that suits the scale of your room. Another plus to this approach is that better than a short-lived bouquet of flowers, containerized shrubs can be moved outdoors to bloom again in your garden or a large container.

Conceal the Plastic Pot

Instead of trying to repot a shrub you bring inside, just slip it into a decorative container that's slightly larger and deeper than the plastic nursery pot. Cover the top with moss to camouflage the rim.

Below: After a long winter, the cheery yellow flowers of a forsythia bush are a welcome sight to color-starved eyes. One of the earliest shrubs to bloom, they are easy to spot in the garden center when the stores open their doors for business in spring.
Opposite: Large round blooms of pink mophead hydrangea shrub make a bold statement that few cut-flower bouquets could rival. Sitting comfortably next to a reading chair that is surrounded by a bird cage and herb pots filled with silver-leafed thyme, tricolor sage, and curly parsley, the bouquet adds the feeling of outdoor freshness to the room.

38. Make a Bold Statement

I must admit that the idea of filling my home with a jungle of tropical houseplants has never held much appeal. But I do enjoy mixing them in my garden borders with more traditional plants. I find tropical plants' bold leaf forms, architectural shapes, and audacious flowers a great way to shake up the mix. They add an exotic spark to gardens that have become a bit too comfortable. Using tropicals in the outdoor garden is nothing new. Plant collectors have grown and collected them for hundreds of years. In fact, many of the annual plants we think of as old-fashioned, such as geraniums, impatiens, and begonias, are actually

tropicals. During Victorian times, these plants were all the rage. Lavish outdoor displays were created during the summer and then these plants were moved into elaborate glass houses to be overwintered for use in next season's garden. This style of gardening was novel and fresh at the time. Its revival today seems to be connected to the interest in creating outdoor living spaces and adding water features to the landscape. There's no better way to give an area a tropical feel than to add plants with huge, shiny leaves, colorful flowers, or ferny textures.

During the warm summer months, you can find an extraordinary range of large, often outrageously so, leaves to bring indoors. Elephant ears, palms, and birds of paradise foliage are a few, but many others exist. This idea of using something bold in a simple way indoors has great appeal. Just as the leaves add a jolt to a garden setting, the foliage also creates a stir in a calm, otherwise complacent living room by drawing your eye to its form as a newly introduced feature. Also, for me, it invites closer examination of these wondrous gifts from nature. Have you ever seen the pattern of an elephant ear as cast against bright sunlight? This alone is awe inspiring. Rather than haul in an entire plant, judiciously harvest a few leaves from plants in your garden or those you may be growing on your porch, deck, or in your house and let them live large displayed in a water-filled vessel. For a list of big-leafed plants, see "Big-Foliage Plants" in the Resource Guide, page 216.

Above: A grouping of several tropical houseplants, including a Chinese fan palm, umbrella plant, white bird of paradise, and ti plant, acts to soften the corner of the living room. When combining several plants together, choose those with contrasting shapes, colors, and sizes.
Opposite: Single leaves of a Chinese fan palm, each displayed in its own glass bottle, create a beautiful focal point in the room.

HARVEST YOUR HOUSEPLANTS

Instead of turning to your flower bed or florist to supply you with materials for garden-themed displays, why not prune some leaves from your tropical houseplants? All it takes is just a few snips and you'll have enough material to make an impressive arrangement.

Houseplants

Hand pruners or heavy scissors

Simple vases with clean lines, such as glass cylinders
or even bud vases, depending on the size

Decorative stones (optional)

1. If you don't already have houseplants with striking foliage, consider adding some to your collection. Be sure to pick ones that will live happily indoors. Appropriate selections for medium- to bright-light plants would be birds of paradise, palms, dracaenas, crotons, tree philodendrons, monstera, and sword ferns. For tough low-light conditions, consider sansevieria, aspidistra, lady palm, and aglaonema.

2. Using pruning shears or heavy scissors, cut a few leaves from your houseplants, pruning them back to the base of the plant on stems that have a single leaf. If your plants are small or don't have much foliage, harvest only a leaf or two to keep from damaging the plant or setting it back. Leaves can be harvested from several different plants if more leaves are needed.

3. Fill a vase with water and arrange the leaves in the vase. If needed, decorative stones placed in the bottom of the vase help anchor top-heavy leaves and give the vase more stability.

Done!

39. *Make a Lasting Impression*

There seem to be two categories of dried flower arrangements: those that are gathered during the late summer, dried, and displayed in the house for a few weeks in fall and early winter as reminders of the harvest and all of its bounty; and those I refer to as the "forever" bouquets, which hang around the house for years. I have a large arrangement in my living room that falls into the latter group. Each fall, I give it a little refresher when I replace some of the stems that are looking weary. I've forgotten when it began its reign, but it works so well with the decor that I can't seem to bring myself to part with it. From a color perspective it is essentially all shades of brown and gold, composed of plants that have dried naturally and taken on this range of tones. I have purposefully avoided dried plants with colorful flower heads, choosing to keep it more monochromatic. On a practical note, I find I get carried away using ornamental grass plumes and that they can, over time, open and shatter, spreading hundreds of their little airborne seeds adrift. I've found the remedy is to spray the plumes with hair spray as they are arranged. This keeps them in check. For lists of plants that keep their form when dried, see "Flowers for Drying" and "Grasses, Plumes, and Leaves for Drying" in the Resource Guide, page 220.

drying blooms and foliage

Dried flowers can make a long-lasting impression throughout the house, complementing any style and decor. For more contemporary spaces, tightly banded sheaths of wheat or barley work well with linear, clean lines, and generous bundles of dried lavender also fit easily in contemporary homes as well as French- and Italian-inspired rooms. Dried alliums and garlic heads offer the same bold, edited look that is often required to harmonize with contemporary styles. More exuberant displays can be created by combining a range of blooms, foliage, and grass plumes gathered from the garden in colors that harmonize with your home's interior colors. Brown corn, dried hydrangea blooms, strawflowers, and a world of dried seed heads and fruit can make strong displays that are natural alternatives to artificial bouquets.

My drying techniques are simple. As I harvest the desired plants, I cut about ten to fifteen at a time with the longest stems possible. I strip away unnecessary leaves and bind each bundle together with a large rubber band. Then all that's needed is to hang the bundles upside-down from the rafters in my garage where it is, for the most part, cool and dry. As the stems dehydrate and shrink, the rubber band continues to tighten and hold the stems together. Once the plants are completely dehydrated they are ready to be put to work.

When you're ready to put an arrangement together, it's best to keep the dried plants bundled rather than try to break them apart into individual stems. And keep in mind that bold groups or splashes of the same plant can make a more visually compelling display.

Opposite: The arrangement follows the same three-shape rule I use in my outdoor container designs. Spikes of mullein (*Verbascum*), black millet, and miscanthus grass give the dried bouquet its tall and spiky form. Dried flowerheads of 'PeeGee' hydrangeas and alliums add a round and full element to the middle of the display. Arching plumes of fountain grass and Sweet Annie (*Artemisia annua*) lend a cascading effect.

PLANT COLLECTIONS

Berries and Seedpods

The garden not only provides glorious flowers to adorn arrangements but also a plethora of berries and seedpods. The value of these types of textures and forms to interior accents cannot be overstated. From a young age I helped my grandmother gather bittersweet vines and rose hips to decorate her fall bouquets. Even then the extra dimension their forms added to the display was clear to me. It gave me an appreciation for the role they played in adding visual interest to arrangements. Since then I look for plants that bear any kind of berries and seedpods, even the humblest roadside plants such as milkweed and chokecherry, as well as garden plants that produce interesting seed heads such as echinacea and broomcorn, to add a layer of subtle grandeur to displays.

1. 'White Dawn' rose hips (Rosa *spp.*)
2. American beautyberry (Callicarpa americana)
3. 'Big Sky Harvest Moon' coneflower seed heads (Echinacea *hybrids*)
4. Okra (Abelmoschus esculentus)
5. Poppy pods (Papaver *spp.*)
6. 'Silver King' artemisia (Artemisia ludoviciana)
7. Lotus seedpod (Nelumbo nucifera)
8. Carolina moonseed (Cocculus carolinus)
9. Love-in-a-mist seedpods (Nigella damascena)

HARVEST HOME DISPLAY

Fall offers an abundance of plants to use in and around your home. During the harvest season it's fun to create displays that symbolize that abundance. While chrysanthemums, pumpkins, and cornstalks are the classic fall decorations used to adorn many front doors, I enjoy the challenge of finding plants that are a fun twist on that theme, such as broomcorn, a type of sorghum that is used for making brooms. It differs from other sorghums in that it produces heads with fibrous seed branches that may be as long as 36 inches. While you might not be able to grow this plant in your garden, look for it at farmers' markets or find other types of fall grasses to create your own one-of-a-kind fall display.

Stalks of red broomcorn (*Sorghum bicolor*)	Roll of brown garden twine
Hand pruners	Stand

1. Gather the broomcorn. If growing in the garden, cut to harvest the longest stalks possible, and then assemble the group so that the seed heads are all at the same level.
2. Wrap twine around the bundle several times to hold it together, tight and secure. Wrap the bundle at the top, middle, and bottom. Trim ends of stalks with pruners so they are all at the same level and will rest flat on the floor.
3. The bundle can be leaned against a wall, or slide it onto a pole stand to keep it upright and more stable.

Done!

Tip: *If you are using a very large bundle of broomcorn, make it easier to handle by creating several smaller bunches and then combining them into one large bundle.*

collections | CAST IRON

Cast iron made its big debut into gardens in the mid-nineteenth century as a result of the Industrial Revolution. No longer were garden ornaments restricted to carved stone or wrought (forged) iron. Machine castings of a single-carved object could be made multiple times over. This made cast-iron railings, balustrades, lampposts, statues, urns, and all forms of garden decoration available and affordable to a growing middle class eager to emulate an aristocratic lifestyle with all of its trappings.

I find my cast-iron containers to be ideal not only for their intended use as planters but as focal points in the center of gar-den pools or indoors as containers for centerpieces or to anchor a corner of a room. Mind you, these colossi of the container world can support entire young trees, mature agave, or armloads of spring boughs. They are great for creating dramatic effect. Their sheer physical size and visual weight offer you the opportunity to think big and "run the limbs up through the chandeliers," as one of my old decorator friends once said. When used inside they can be painted any color but will need solid support if placed on a table. I have found kitchen trivets and cork-bottom hot pads to be good protectors for furniture.

The gray-green colors of the two Jarrahdale pumpkins, the hubbard squash, and the ghost plant (*Grapto-petalum paraguayense*) harmonize beautifully with the floor in front of the fireplace, while adding visual interest with their intriguing shapes and textures. Jarrahdale pumpkins are from Australia and have an orange-colored flesh that is sweet, nutty, and stringless, so it's great for baking. Many ornamental pumpkins are fun to look at but not very good to eat, but this one is very tasty. The ghost plant is a succulent from Mexico that is quite drought-tolerant and takes temperatures as low as 18 degrees F.

40. Plant a Mini-Garden

I enjoyed making terrariums as a kid and I still do today. It is one of the best ways to introduce children to gardening and give them an understanding of nature's life cycles and systems. More than a science project, these terrariums can be stylish additions to any room either as large single elements or as clusters of several varied shapes.

Certainly the larger the container, the larger the "canvas" you have to apply your creativity. Look for plants that are small leafed and slow growing. Also, if the jar has a lid, choose plants that can take high humidity. Fuzzy-leaved plants are usually not the best candidates for terrariums, as they are more prone to rot.

Terrariums are simple to put together: just add a couple of inches of gravel to the bottom of the jar, layer in some aquarium charcoal (to absorb odors), add sterilized potting soil, and then plant. Mist the sides of the jar to remove any unwanted soil and water so the soil is moist, but not soggy. When covered and placed in bright, indirect light, you won't need to water the contents of the terrarium again for several months. Talk about your low-maintenance houseplants! I like to make several terrariums and arrange them in groups of three or more. Choosing containers with complementary shapes and varying heights adds interest to the display.

For lists of plants that will grow well in the humid environment of a terrarium, see "Plants for Terrariums" in the Resource Guide, page 209.

Left and Opposite: In terrariums with lids, moisture will appear on the inside of the jar as water evaporates and condenses on the sides, simulating a miniature rainforest. Be sure to select plants that enjoy that type of environment. Avoid placing a sealed terrarium in direct sun, as the plants risk overheating. And since you want the plants to stay small, use very little fertilizer. Water only when you see the sides of the glass are dry and no moisture is evident in the jar.

At one time bedrooms and baths were located in different areas of our homes, separated by a long walk down the hall and shared by others. Today the rooms are often blended into a master suite—a private place to go to rest, restore, and refuel for a new day. While the bedroom is still meant for sleeping, it can also be a place to stretch out and watch TV, read a book, exercise, set up a home office, or meditate. And when it comes to adding accents to create a feel of a personal sanctuary, items like fresh flowers, sweet-smelling sachets, cheerful houseplants, and even a touch of whimsy can become part of what makes your sanctuary truly special. Because the area serves as a haven, garden-inspired accents help to add an extra layer of pampering amenities to make you feel like you've indulged yourself just a bit.

Bedroom and Bath

Bathrooms, which were once called "necessary rooms," no longer need to be cold and sterile places. In earlier times, they were asked to serve only our basic needs with little fanfare, but now their roles, like those of our bedrooms, have expanded in size and luxuries. Sure, the room must be functional, but it is also the perfect place to add garden-themed touches to help add color and soften the hard lines of fixtures and counters. The warm, humid conditions are ideal for growing an indoor plant. And the fragrance of garden flowers adds a relaxed, down-to-earth ambience to the room.

Ever since my childhood, sleeping outdoors surrounded by all the sights and sounds of nature held great appeal. It always felt like it was a special adventure when I could spend the night in a tent or even on a sleeping porch. As an adult, I have come to enjoy my creature comforts, but I still want to have that outdoor feel in the bedrooms and baths in my home. I've found that one of the biggest hurdles I've had to overcome is my habit of creating flower arrangements and seasonal displays more for the public areas of my home and overlooking the bedroom and bath. I'm sure it's a throwback to the idea that when company is on the way, you put out your best and always add a bouquet of cut flowers for the table. So recently I've been making an effort to treat myself as a welcomed guest and give these more private areas of my home the same level of garden style that I add to my kitchen, living room, and dining room. In doing so, I've noticed how much more I enjoy being in these rooms. To me, it's almost like the difference between a yard of mowed grass and one that is filled with the fragrance and beauty of a colorful garden. Adding garden accents gives me a reason to slow down and appreciate the magic that a touch of nature brings to the rooms. I invite you to try it for yourself and see what a difference it makes.

Opposite, clockwise from top left: Simple and soothing, the rosette-shaped leaves of the sedum purple 'Afterglow' echeveria make the perfect bedside accent; the flower-like form of this easy-care houseplant gives the bedroom a garden-style touch. What better way to soak in the beauty of the garden than in a warm bubble bath on a screen porch; a large potted agapanthus sits at the foot of the tub to help blur the lines between indoors and out. A framed print of vegetables and a simple houseplant add a touch of the garden to this bedside stand. A few stout branches is all that's needed to make this fun and easy clothes hanger; painted birdhouses perched on the horizontal support add a touch of whimsy.

41. Add One Touch

I believe that plants heal our spirits. Whether we are kneeling to plant seeds in a garden, tending to house-plants, or arranging flowers in a vase, plants feed our souls with subtle energies, providing visual nourishment and soothing fragrances. They are my connection to the earth's rhythms and a way to stay in touch with forces greater than myself. For that reason and more, I've found a plant next to the bed to be a comforting agent. It is there to remind me of the greater garden outdoors, my role in its care, and its value to my life. A single houseplant on a nightstand is all it takes.

My selection often hinges on finding a plant that coordinates with the colors in the room. I've lost count of the times I've gone into a paint store with a leaf or bloom from the garden with the idea of finding a matching color chip. I've found it isn't as easy as you might think. The greens, for some reason, are particularly hard to find an exact match for. However, when I'm selecting plants for the house that will harmonize with the existing color scheme in a room, it seems easier. The colors in the foliage and blooms are more forgiving and accommodating than paint. Using a plant to pick up on an accent color in the room really brings a room to life. My choice varies with the seasons, but often I'm drawn to an easy-care houseplant that is content to quietly reside in the varied light conditions of the room. I find its steady presence a welcome comfort.

Opposite: The beauty of this plant is in its double-duty nature. 'Campfire' sedum (*Crassula coccinea*) is as comfortable indoors as out. It can be used in landscapes, in succulent combinations, or as a houseplant. The striking coloration and interesting form make this particular succulent stand out from the rest.

practical tips for watering plants

When you bring the garden indoors, whether it is in the form of cut flowers or living plants, the conditions you place them in can make a big impact on their longevity and success. I am often asked about how much and when to water plants indoors. Of course, there are a number of factors involved, but some basic tips may serve as guidelines.

First, regarding cut flowers, look for every opportunity to keep them hydrated. If harvesting them from your garden, cut them early in the morning and place immediately into a plastic bucket filled with water as you cut them. Once inside, transfer the flowers to a tall bucket with cool, fresh water all the way up to the throat of the blossom. Keep them in a cool, dark place until you are ready to arrange them. Once arranged, keep the vessel full of water. I recommend a commercial preservative and food source for cut flowers because it can actually help extend the life of the flowers. Change the water in glass containers every two to four days, and add fresh preservative, too.

As you may know, actually getting the water into the arrangement on a regular basis can present its own challenges. I've found that ice cubes placed at the base of the flowers and allowed to melt is an old trick that works, and don't forget a turkey baster can also come in handy getting water to those difficult-to-reach places without spilling all over the dining-room table.

As for potted plants, I divide them into two categories: those that can sustain themselves for long periods without water in their natural environment and those that need to have their roots remain consistently moist.

The first category includes plants like agaves, aloes, cacti, Haworthias, and even the rugged snake plant. These require little water as houseplants and in fact insist on moisture in moderation; otherwise the roots will rot. I would also add bromeliads and orchids to this list because of the way they take in moisture in their native habitats. Allow all of these to go completely dry before giving them a soak.

For the others, keep the soil consistently moist and use the "finger test." Stick your finger in the soil to see if it feels dry, and if so, water the plant. If it feels moist, leave it alone for a few days. From spring through fall, use a very diluted all-purpose fertilizer so the plants get a light feeding each time you water. This seems to work well particularly for those that produce flowers.

42. Grow a Bouquet

Each fall, I plant my flower beds with a variety of spring-flowering bulbs such as tulips, daffodils, crocuses, alliums, and snowdrops, to name a few. Along with planting bulbs in my garden, I also like to pot some in containers. Black plastic nursery pots are ideal for this and a great way to reuse the containers. Since most spring-flowering bulbs require several weeks of cold weather to stimulate their growth, the pots make good outdoor planters until they begin to bloom. I keep an eye on them outside through the winter and just before the flowers open in the spring, I bring them into my bedroom and slip them into a more decorative container that is large enough to conceal the nursery pot.

Now, I like the look of a container spilling over with tulips, so here's my method. In the fall I find a large nursery pot—one about 20 inches in diameter. Then I gather up at least seventy-five tulip bulbs, all of the same variety and color. You may prefer to create a different mix, but be aware that tulips are designed to bloom either in early, mid-, or late spring. So if you are going to mix varieties, make sure they all have the same bloom time.

The next step is to fit seventy-five bulbs in a 20-inch container. To do that, they need to be layered. Tulips are like prepackaged flowers. They don't really draw much nutrition from the soil, but they do need good drainage. Be sure your container has drainage holes and then add some small stones, gravel, or broken pot pieces in the bottom. You want to prevent the roots from coming out of the hole but not the water. Next, add enough soil so when it is pressed down, the soil surface is about 14 to 16 inches below the top of the container. Pack in twenty-five bulbs, shoulder to shoulder, as the first layer. Add more soil until just the tips of the bulbs are showing and then layer in another twenty-five bulbs on top. Avoid planting a bulb over the tip of a bulb on the first level. Add another layer of soil and the last twenty-five bulbs, and then fill the rest of the container with soil.

To bloom, bulbs need at least 15 weeks of cold, but not freezing, temperatures. If you live in an area where winter temperatures stay below freezing, keep the containers in a sheltered area, unheated garage, or shed to keep them from freezing. Bulbs in containers are more susceptible to weather extremes than those in the ground. If that's not an option, you can wrap the container in burlap or Bubble Wrap or even between bales of hay. In very warm climates, keep the containers out of the sun and top them off with mulch to help keep them cool. No matter your climate, keep the containers watered through the winter. When spring comes, place the plastic nursery pot in a bright-light area. When a container of tulips blooms, it is literally a living bouquet and a knockout display to have in your bedroom.

Opposite: Wouldn't you love to wake up to this beautiful bouquet of 'White Parrot' tulips in your bedroom? Parrot tulips are different from the standard cup-shaped tulip blossoms in that their petals are feathered, curled, or waved, making them a dramatic standout.

Tulip Tips

Purchase high-quality bulbs without soft spots or mold.

The larger the bulb size, the bigger the flower.

Tulips are hardy in USDA Zones 3–7.

In warmer areas, chill the bulbs before planting by refrigerating them for 8 weeks at 40 to 45 degrees F.

Prechilled bulbs are also available to purchase.

If planted in the ground, place bulbs 6–8 inches deep.

43. Build a Clothes Rack with Branches

Gardeners are often thought of as practical people. That would be true of most of the gardeners I know. I think it's a trait that develops as time and experience teaches us all that goes with tending plants. As you garden, you gain a set of basic skills so you know when it's time to prune, sow seeds, weed, and water and how to care for a garden's needs as it grows and develops. And whether we are willing to admit it or not, we are also artists. Why else would we try year after year to paint pictures with plants on a constantly changing and often inhospitable canvas? I like to think of gardening as painting with a very broad brush, and the really wonderful thing about it is that if it doesn't work, nature gives me a new canvas to try again.

Another aspect of gardening that one can't help but notice is the economy of nature. Recycling and reusing is a basic premise found in the natural world and one that encourages me to be frugal with resources. So whenever I can find a project that lets me use both my practical and artistic sides as well as recycle items in nature, I see it as a fun and creative challenge. For example, one of my favorite activities to share with elementary school children is to go for a short hike and let each student collect a small bag of items found along the way. They like to pick up small twigs, leaves, dried plants, feathers, and seeds such as acorns. It's like a treasure hunt of goodies from nature. Then we take the items back into the classroom and they glue them to cardboard picture frames. The embellishments delight and intrigue the children and help them to see at an early age how they can enhance their lives with nature-inspired projects. I hope it's a memory they carry with them as they grow.

SECURE FASTENERS

When constructing this clothes hanger with tree branches, use limbs at least 1 inch in diameter. Drill a small "pilot" hole where a fastener will be used to hold the branches together. Use wood screws to attach the limbs and then wrap a lightweight wire around the joints for added strength. Use dry wood only for crosspieces and other straight pieces. If the wood is freshly cut, it will shrink as it dries, so you may need to tighten the joints as shrinkage occurs.

As adults we can create similar projects on a larger scale and use natural objects to give interior spaces a feeling of outdoors. In a bedroom there is always a need for more places to hang clothes and personal belongings. Creating a clothes rack from backyard branches is a great solution. Add some birdhouses as embellishments to give it a touch of whimsy.

When you are searching for garden-inspired accessories to add to your bedrooms and bath, consider looking around to see what's available in your garden or shed. You may discover just the right treasure to create a one-of-a-kind accent that is not only fun and fanciful but useful, too.

44. Press Plants into Service

Pressed flowers and foliage can be transformed into beautifully framed botanical art, though I've found that the outlines of leaves make the most compelling displays. My method is simple: Use scissors or hand pruners to collect the leaves when they are free of dew or rain. If the plants are going to be displayed together, choose those with contrasting shapes and sizes for more visual interest.

Then I create my botanical press. Simply put, a press sandwiches leaves of plants between layers of absorbent material so they will dry quickly. I put a stack of newsprint on a board and arrange the leaves on a page and then lay several sheets of paper on top. More paper and plants can be stacked if you want to press several plants, then top off the stack with another wooden board and weigh it down with something heavy, like a big book, bricks, or a can of paint, and leave it in a warm, dry place. Make sure the plants are completely dry before removing them.

The next step is to mount the plants. A simple and fast way is to use thinned white glue to attach plants to heavy paper. While effective, it isn't as long-lasting as other methods. Since I want my pressed leaves to last for years, I take them to a local shop that does professional picture framing. There the foliage is sewn to a foam board on acid-free paper and a spacer is added to prevent the foliage from touching the glass.

TO MINIMIZE FADING OF PRESSED FOLIAGE

Keep pressed foliage pictures out of rooms with high humidity, such as bathrooms or kitchens, and avoid displaying the pictures in direct sunlight. Try to make an airtight seal when framing; air causes oxidation and premature fading of pressed plants.

Above: By carefully arranging the fern leaves on the newsprint, I can make sure that the foliage will be pressed just as I want it to be displayed in the frame. **Opposite:** Preserved in silver frames is the pressed foliage of a royal fern, acanthus, arborvitae fern, and plume poppy. For a successful arrangement, keep the plants and the frames similar in color and style. I've arranged these four pictures in a staggered pattern. Depending on the number of prints you have they could also have an appeal arranged in straight lines or a checkerboard or random pattern, but keep the pictures close together for the most impact.

45. *Promote Beauty and Rest*

According to the principles of the ancient Chinese practices of feng shui, strategic placement of objects in a house can promote good health and positive feelings. For instance, placing houseplants throughout a home can enhance the flow of energy through the entire dwelling. And houseplants in the bedroom can mean better sleep for the occupants of the house.

Whether these are ideas you practice or not, there's little debate that the green foliage of houseplants helps soften the mood of a room. It can mute harsh lines, endow a bare window with charm, or add a touch of symmetry to oddly furnished walls. In general, houseplants lend a pleasant, soothing effect to the bedroom that promotes relaxation and sleep. Now while this information may not make the headlines in the local paper, what you may be surprised to learn is that houseplants have some real health benefits that go beyond aesthetic appeal. They also absorb odors and fumes, replenish the air with oxygen and humidity, and keep the temperatures cool and conducive for better sleep.

To enjoy the benefits of houseplants in your bedroom, keep a few basic tips in mind. If you are "green thumb challenged" start with some small easy-care plants. Not all plants are created equal and some are definitely fussier than others to keep alive. For a list of a few recommended varieties, see "Easy-Care House-plants" in the Resource Guide, page 213.

Before you buy a plant, make sure to select one that's suited to grow in your bedroom's light conditions. If you are gone most days, take note of the light in the room on the weekend to see how much sunlight enters the room through the day. Keep in mind the light changes through the year as well, so you may need to move plants around to make adjustments for the seasons. Many people keep their bedroom windows covered with heavy drapes and blinds to control the light, and unless you open them before you leave, you may not realize how dark the room is when you're gone all day. If the room is located on the north end of your house, chances are there isn't much natural light coming into the room, so a low-light plant would be best suited for those situations. Just check the plant's tag or ask knowledgeable staff at a garden center to find the right plant for you.

If you have a little more experience growing houseplants and are ready for more, try grouping several plants together or go for large-leafed species like dracaena, philodendron, or the banyan tree (*Ficus benghalensis*). If you have a large, sparsely furnished room, they can really fill up the space. Conversely, in a small room, large plants are oppressive and take up way too much space. To get the best effect, you should choose midsized or small plants with large delicate leaves. Put the plants where they are going to be visible. Don't put too many plants in a small space or it will get too crowded and your individual plants won't make their full impact on the room.

Opposite: 'Christmas Bells' white heather (*Erica canaliculata*) has the charming look of a miniature Christmas tree covered in snow. It provides a restful quality to a bedroom setting. Keep the plant in bright light and enjoy its seasonal flowering in spring. It is a tender perennial, so it can grow outdoors but only in the warm areas of the country such as Zones 9 and 10.

Princess pine sedum (*Crassula muscosa pseudolycopodiodes*) is an exotic-looking houseplant that adds a beautiful touch to the bedroom. Like most sedums, it grows best when you let the soil dry out between waterings, and it also likes bright, indirect light near a window. This plant makes a nice counterpoint when combined with large succulent leaves in wreaths and topiaries.

HERBAL MOTH REPELLENT

One of the best uses I've found for herbs is to make an herbal moth repellent. It's a safe and inexpensive way to deal with these household pests that are often found in clothes closets or sweater drawers. You can grow and dry these herbs yourself, or you can find them in health food stores or online. That's also a good place to purchase the oils. Once the ingredients are blended together, make a sachet or fill a jar with a vented lid to put on the shelf in your closet. Sachet bags can be found in craft stores, or you can make your own from cotton fabric.

Large bowl	30 drops of lavender oil
Large spoon for mixing	5 drops of rosemary oil
1 ounce wormwood or artemisia	5 drops of vetiver (grass extract)
4 ounces lavender flowers	Large glass jar with vented lid
2 ounces rosemary leaves	6 2-inch-square sachet bags (optional)
Handful of cedar shavings	

1. In a large bowl, mix together the dried herbs and cedar shavings.

2. Pour the essential oils into the dried herb mixture and gently toss.

3. Fill the glass jar with the mixture. Put a vented lid on the jar and place it where moths are a problem, such as your closet or wardrobe. You can also fill sachet bags with the mixture and put them in your drawers.

Done!

46. Let Foliage Work for You

Too often foliage is passed over by our attraction to blooms. This is certainly the case in the garden and I see the same myopic view inside the home. By embracing foliage you do not in any way sacrifice beauty or color; both are present in a range of forms. The advantage good foliage has over blooms is that it is long lasting. Rather than cycling in and out of flower, the color, pattern, and texture remain a constant.

Another compelling reason to fill your bedroom with foliage houseplants is that they help remove toxins from the air pollutants that are found in houses from industrial chemicals used to manufacture building materials and numerous household cleaners that may contain formaldehyde, benzene, ammonia, acetone, and ethyl acetate. These pollutants are actually absorbed through the leaves of the plants and converted to harmless substances. Experts estimate that fifteen houseplants make a significant impact on improving the air quality in a house. So along with foliage houseplants adding color and texture to your bedroom, they also help clean the air.

For a list of the best air-cleaning plants for your bedroom, see "Air-Cleaning Plants" in the Resource Guide, page 216.

Above left: The heart-shaped intricately patterned leaves of a caladium arise from a container of frilly asparagus ferns. Enjoy caladiums as houseplants in indirect-light settings, and then in late fall the foliage will fade. Store the tubers in a paper bag in a warm, dry place. In late winter, pot the tubers up again, begin watering, and your plants will come back to life. **Above right:** The vivid colors on these crotons make them a focal point in any room. To maintain their richly hued foliage, keep the plant within 3 to 5 feet of a sunny window. **Opposite:** Blending the bushy fronds of 'Myers' foxtail fern with the bold and deeply serrated leaves of a tree philodendron helps to enliven the room. For some, the fern produces tiny white to pink flowers that develop into attractive bright red berries. Seed from the berries can be used to start new plants.

PLANT COLLECTIONS

Houseplants

I must admit, I am only a recent convert to houseplants. For many years I found them rather mundane and the few I had were gifts. Only those that could thrive on my lack of attention had any chance of survival. My friends would often comment that I wasn't representing my profession very well by not taking care of these plants. My conversion was slow. It began as a need to put something in an empty urn or enliven a darkened corner. Gradually I discovered several easy-care plants that brightened my mood as well as my decor. Now they are a welcome addition to my home.

1. *White rabbit's-foot fern (*Humata tyermannii*)*
2. *Chinese jade plant (*Crassula ovata arborescens*)*
3. *Oncidium orchid*
4. *'Afterglow' echeveria (*Echeveria hybrids*)*
5. *'Miami Storm' begonia (*Begonia rex-cultorum*)*
6. *Airplane plant (*Chlorophytum comosum*)*
7. *Croton (*Codiaeum variegatum*)*
8. *Peace lily (*Spathiphyllum wallisii*)*
9. *Echeveria (*Echeveria nodulosa*)*

47. Make a Medley

A florist once told me that "too much is just enough" as he was preparing some massive bouquets for the Metropolitan Museum of Art. This catchphrase has resonated with me from time to time. I think there is a lot we can learn about garden design and container gardening through talented florists, and I might add the information flow goes both ways. Many of the basic principles of design translate well to both gardeners and florists.

I often take a florist's approach when trying to create the "wow factor" with houseplants. Heaping masses of them together in a single concentrated place can yield eye-popping results. And by making good choices, the composition will last for months, or until you become weary of it and want to see some change. A good place to start is to treat houseplants like cut flowers and apply some of the same techniques as you would to an arrangement. Avoid getting too elaborate by following this rule of thumb: use three contrasting plants that "play well" together. A design balance I try to achieve is two-thirds foliage plants to one-third flowers. Then I group them together generously in clusters in a single large container. I found the perfect spot of this medley of foliage plants in the bedroom, but this arrangement could be used in several places throughout the house.

Opposite: This lively mix of houseplants blends the golden yellow and bronze flowers of a kalanchoe with the long, slender, grasslike leaves of a Madagascar dragon tree, the vining quality of a creeping fig, the distinctive white and green markings on 'Sylvie' ficus, and the white-veined foliage of the arrowhead vine.

CLEANING HOUSEPLANTS

Dust can diminish a plant's ability to breathe, so wipe hard-surfaced leaves by supporting them with one hand and swabbing the surface with a soft cloth and tepid water. Fuzzy or prickly leaves such as African violets or cacti should be cleaned with a soft brush.

I find that plants generally look best against simple backgrounds. But if you do want to mix it up, go for contrast between the plant and the walls by placing plants with large foliage in front of wallpaper with a small pattern, for example. If you have large-patterned wallpaper, achieve contrast with fine leaves such as a fern. Use the light entering the room to your advantage. Go for plants that will cast interesting or unusual patterns on the floors, walls, and ceilings if there is a time of the day when they are backlit by the sun.

Make sure the colors of leaves and flowers you choose coordinate with your bedroom's decor. You don't want the look of your home's furnishings and wall coverings diminished by the wrong-colored houseplants. And follow the same rule of thumb as you would when placing flowers in a garden border—put larger plants behind smaller ones. I also like to be sure the edge of a container is softened with a few leaves or cascading plants spilling over the edge.

48. Adopt a No-Fail Houseplant

Often, when I'm introduced to people as a garden designer, the first thing I hear is "I can't grow a thing! I can't even keep my houseplants alive." For all you intrepid gardeners, I say make it easy on yourself and start out with something that is downright hard to kill. There are some plants that seem to thrive on abuse; and I know this from firsthand experience, because they are the type of plants I like the best! One of my favorite plants with this indestructible quality is commonly known as mother-in-law's tongue or snake plant, or if you want a formal introduction, its botanical name is *Sansevieria trifasciata*. And while many a mother-in-law may cringe at the comparison, one look at the plant and you can see how it came by that common name. Snake plants became popular across the United States in the 1920s and 1930s because they were one of the plants, along with African violets, that Woolworth stores sold. The Florida foliage plant industry had its start growing these plants for distribution to that chain.

A MODERN TWIST

Designers are rediscovering the snake plant's striking futuristic look. Try the plant in a large stainless-steel square container for a contemporary style, or in a vintage planter for a more retro look.

The plant is perfect for the bedroom, as it can survive in about as low a light level as you would encounter in the home. Although it may not grow much in really dimly lit recesses, it will sit there just the same and, with an occasional dusting, will look as good as the day it was placed there. It doesn't need a lot of water, and fertilization is optional, at least when the plant is inside. If you want your plant to grow, move it to the patio in the summer and give it an occasional shot of fertilizer and an occasional watering. And here's more good news about the plant: it loves to be rootbound, so there's no need to worry about transplanting it. Place it in a bold container to complement its strong straight lines.

Opposite: Often the snake plant is found in homes tucked away in a dark corner of a room. But I find it is best enjoyed on top of a table or dresser, elevated to eye level, where the patterns on its foliage can be appreciated and its long vertical form can add height and drama to a room. There are several new varieties of this old favorite that may be an even better match to your bedroom's decor. Among the tall types, 'Black Gold' has leaves that are deep green edged with yellow, 'Golden Coral' has reticulated patterns that are variegated with a yellow margin, and 'Moonshine' is a light, silver-leafed variety.

49. Redefine Dishware

I recall a garden-themed birthday brunch I attended a few years ago. At each place setting the hostess had a cup and saucer filled with flowering annuals planted in the cups. All the dishes were different shapes, colors, and patterns. It was a delightfully carefree touch that made an impression on me.

I enjoy experiences that offer a new way to use a common object. They always inspire me to shake things up and try an unconventional approach in decorating and entertaining. Why not plates covered in turf to serve as chargers for a golfer's big-five-oh party? Or platters with tiny gardens planted on them as centerpieces? In fact, why should dishware be confined to the dining room? I find commodious soup tureens to be wonderful accents in the bedroom, inviting a world of plant possibilities from the garden. Using dishes this way is an unexpected way to add a touch of the garden to the bedroom.

Above: The soup tureen from my set of brown transferware holds a bright bouquet of spring-flowering daffodils and summer snowflakes (*Leucojum aestivum*). Since the stems of the daffodils and snowflakes are hollow, the trick to getting the flowers to stand up in the tureen is to cover the opening with some chicken wire. The openings in the wire provide support for the stems and allow the blossoms to be easily positioned in the right direction. Chicken wire can be purchased from your local home improvement store and cut with heavy scissors or wire cutters. Carefully bend the corners to fit the mouth of the container and then pack in the blooms to conceal the wire.

No matter where I travel, I am constantly looking for containers for plants. My appreciation for transferware started precisely this way. Transferware is the product of the Industrial Revolution, reaching its zenith of popularity in the nineteenth century. It did not require hand-painting, as images were "transferred" from copper-plate engravings onto ceramic. This process allowed it to be made more efficiently and affordably. It represented "style for the people," affordable table-ware for the growing middle class in England and America.

I bought a rather knocked-around piece in a Bath, England, flea market for a little more than three pounds sterling. It was a square covered vegetable dish. What caught my eye, besides the price, was that it still had the attached saucer intact, which made it perfect for a potted plant. And as fate would have it, the seller was a landscape historian and garden designer. From this purchase of my first piece of transferware, a lifelong international friendship was struck. Since then, I have added pieces as I found them, from soup tureens and plates to the odd cup and saucer. No piece is from the same set, yet they all hang together harmoniously.

I am also drawn to transferware for its depiction of eighteenth- and nineteenth-century landscape themes. Some of the scenes on the dishes depict specific landscapes of note, but more often than not they are generic themes or vignettes that focus on a single object; all offer some insight into the way our ancestors looked at the landscape and garden. One of my favorites is an old soup bowl with a large ceremonial garden urn as its subject. Transferware can be found in a range of colors, including various shades of blue, black, red, green, and so on. I have always collected brown because it is neutral, and with it you can lay a splendid autumn table.

50. Add Some Charm

To me, whether it is in the garden or in a home, the unexpected and whimsical are always welcome. I enjoy visiting someone's house and picking up on elements of their lighter side. I find it refreshing and these surprising touches offer a glimpse of another part of their personality. Frankly, it would be nice to see more of this. Too often we take our gardens, homes, and what we wear way too seriously. Now, I'm not suggesting that you create a three-ring circus in your house or have a life-sized cut-out of Jerry Seinfeld in your living room (although if he was holding a potted plant, it might be kind of fun). Whimsy can be achieved by using interesting containers, plants in surprising places, like the bathroom, or bits of garden ornament used in clever ways. How about a rubber ducky as a planter or goldfish in a bowl? My view of a garden home has lots of fun elements—an umbrella stand full of pink flamingos, a collection of ceramic pigs, or plants that look like hair growing from stone sculptures.

EXPERIMENT

When it comes to adding elements of fun to the bath, don't be afraid to move objects around until you find the right piece. Decorating is a subjective, intuitive process that requires some trial and error. Move items in and live with them for a while. You'll know when you've found just the right piece.

Above right: Add personality plus a touch of the garden to the bathroom. The weathered stone head sports a froth of green foliage that looks like unkempt hair. The maidenhair fern (*Adiantum capillus-veneris*) is well suited for the bathroom's humid environment. To create the same soil conditions as the fern enjoys in its native environment, mix commercial potting soil with compost and leaf mold in a 50/25/25 percent ratio.

51. Fill the Room with Fragrance

Personally, when it comes to adding fragrance to a home's interior, I prefer the perfume of flowers over aerosol sprays or scented candles. Plant-derived aromas just have more appeal to me. I've discovered that fragrance is not so much a science as it is a memory. It seems that we learn to associate smells with an event or feeling. That explains why two people will rarely have the same reaction to a scent—with perhaps the exception of the aroma of an apple pie baking in the oven. Who can call that smell anything but heavenly?

There is no classification of scents other than vague descriptions that range from pleasant to unpleasant and that vary greatly from person to person. An aroma that I find intoxicating may not smell so sweet to another. We seem to have a library of plant aromas in our heads so that when someone says "honeysuckle," we nod in recognition of what that means. Other familiar fragrances include roses, mint, a smoky fire, newly mown grass, or the air after a rain. But a garden is more than a single aroma; it is a mixture of a thousand scents carried on the breeze of a day.

Inside the house, I like to have several small vases close at hand that I can find in a moment's notice to fill with aromatic plants. Placing these around the house, particularly when I'm having guests, is a simple way to enliven a bathroom vanity or bedside nightstand, or to accent the breakfast table. Their diminutive size ensures that all that's required to fill them is plucking a few blooms, leaves, or herbs, which only takes a few minutes, so the effect is much greater than the time spent. It is amazing how transforming a touch of the garden can be to a space. I like to mix the fragrance of plants with colorful leaves such as begonias, Persian shield, and fern fronds to further enhance the senses. Herbs such as lemongrass, rosemary, lavender, and mint add a subtle but pleasant fragrance to the room. In a small bathroom all it takes is a tiny cluster of orange or lemon blooms or a single gardenia to fill the space with perfume.

Left: The fresh sweet scent from these Calamondin orange blossoms in small stone vases quickly fills the bathroom. History tells us that France's King Louis XIV so loved the aroma that he had the first orangerie built to have the trees bloom year-round. After enjoying their intoxicating fragrance, you'll understand his passion.

52. *Select a Flower with Staying Power*

Too often we fall into a pattern of thinking that bringing a beautiful bouquet of flowers into our homes should be reserved for special occasions, and that for our day-to-day lives, such things are extravagances or just too much trouble to deal with. Okay, I'll fess up, I'm describing my habits to a tee. And yet when I think about the rooms where I would notice and appreciate these touches the most, it would be the bedroom or bathroom. After all, they are both places where we do spend time every day. Here's where the splendor of the orchid comes to our rescue. Not only is this plant a symbol of nature's most beautiful acts of perfection, but it is well suited to the bathroom. Orchids are easy to care for, take low light, and adore the higher humidity the bathroom offers. Best of all, they bloom for a very long time. Also, in bathrooms we often are limited to small ledges to place things on, and orchids can be grown in very small containers. I prefer shatterproof containers in the bathroom to avoid the chance of broken glass.

For too long orchids have been labeled as plants that are difficult to grow and too expensive or too exotic for most people's homes, but happily those descriptions are being debunked. More and more people are growing orchids because they are readily available and less expen-

PRETTY PROPS

I go for understated ways to support the blooms of flowering houseplants. Lichen-covered twigs or slender green bamboo stakes make inconspicuous props to keep the regal blooms of orchids aloft.

sive than they have been in the past. If you compare the price of the plant with the duration of bloom, you can see that they're actually a very good value.

One of the easiest orchids to grow is the phalaenopsis. It will tolerate low-light conditions, and as far as the ideal temperature goes, if you're comfortable, it is too. When it comes to soil, orchids really don't need any at all. They prefer the bark of fir trees. Some growers like to create an orchid-growing medium by blending fir bark and lava rock. Orchids are light eaters. You only need to fertilize them with just a quarter of the label-recommended amount and then only every other week. One thing you do need to watch for is salt buildup from fertilizer, so once a month or so let water run through the growing medium to wash that out. When the plant is content, those gorgeous flowers will look fresh for about two months. After the blooms fade, cut the stalk above the second or third node and reduce fertilizing to once a month.

Opposite: Once you've soaked in a warm tub, taking in the beauty of an orchid such as this pink moth orchid (*Phaelanopsis*), you'll look forward to your next opportunity to repeat this relaxing pleasure. The meditative quality of these hypnotic beauties is legendary. No wonder orchid collectors have gone to the ends of the earth to find new varieties.

SHELF WITH FERN

Adding a shelf under a high window in the bathroom creates the perfect out-of-the way place for a plant. Here, the chrome shelf with towel hooks matches the fixtures in the room. A bird's nest fern, still in its plastic nursery pot, sits inside the ice bucket. The bucket, lined with a plastic bag that is filled with about 3 inches of gravel, serves as a decorative holder for the fern. When the plant is watered, the moisture drains through the plant and is collected in the gravel.

Shelf	Decorative plant container
Brackets	Aquarium gravel
Screwdriver	Plastic liner (large Ziploc bag)
Screws	Plant

1. Install a shelf below a window with good light.

2. Choose a decorative holder for the plant. If it doesn't have drainage holes, such as this ice bucket, create a lining by adding a couple of inches of aquarium gravel to the bottom of a water-tight plastic bag and slip it inside the container. The gravel keeps the plant above any collected water and provides additional height so the plant doesn't sit too low in the bucket.

3. Place the plant on top of the gravel. Adjust the level of the gravel as needed so the plant sits at the right height in the container. Place the container with the plant on the shelf.

Done!

53. *Make a Microclimate*

Many plants that enjoy living indoors are tropical natives and prefer a higher level of humidity than might otherwise be found in our homes, particularly during the fall and winter when the air becomes dry because of home heating. Certain rooms are more hospitable to plants because of the higher humidity they offer. Bathrooms are best because of the daily dose of steamy vapor from our baths and showers. Kitchens, too, can offer an increase in humidity particularly over a sink.

For those plants that benefit from higher air moisture, you can create little microclimates for a single plant. Start with an oversized saucer, one at least twice the diameter of the plant's container, and fill it with pea-sized gravel up to a quarter of an inch from the top of the saucer. Place the plant on the gravel bed, and then just keep it filled with water. As the water evaporates, it will bathe the underside of the leaves with moisture.

For lots of smaller containers it's helpful to use a large rectangular pan or tray and take the same approach, only this time clustering the containers together on one tray. You will be doing them a favor and creating a great-looking display at the same time.

Opposite and below: Plants such as this lemon button fern (*Nephrolepis cordifolia* 'Duffi') thrive in the humid conditions of a bathroom. The compact plant stays under 12 inches tall and will send out runners that sprout new plants. When it is actively growing it has a very subtle but clear lemon scent, giving the bathroom a fresh aroma. The fern grows best near a north or east window. Avoid a location where it would have direct sun on it in the afternoon.

Whether it's a casual brunch on the patio, a backyard barbecue with friends, or a formal dinner under a blanket of stars, it's hard to beat the romance of an outdoor meal. Dining in a fresh-air setting is an invitation for Mother Nature to add her own special qualities to the experience with soft breezes, sweet birdsongs, and the perfume of the earth. As temperatures allow, I try to enjoy as many outdoor meals as possible. Food just tastes better in the fresh air. The setting is a naturally sociable place. Even when dining by yourself, you are never alone. It takes only a few minutes of sitting quietly at my table on the loggia to notice all the activity in my garden: birds, bees, butterflies, and, of course, Marge the cat. When family and friends join me the meals take on a relaxed atmosphere. In the garden there's little need for all the formalities; children

Outdoor Dining

can scatter crumbs and no one seems to be in such a hurry. After dark, the setting becomes a place of mystery and romance, lit by votives and lanterns.

I've found the key to designing an outdoor setting is much the same as the approach I use to create the interior of my own home. I think of the sky and the canopy of trees as the ceiling; fences, shrubs, flower beds, and containers as the walls; and the grass, bricks, or decking as the floor. The vista beyond the room serves as windows, and gates, arches, and arbors, become welcoming entries. Thought of this way, positioning the table, chairs, and decorative features seems easier to imagine. Then all the wonderful elements of light and shadow, flowers, herbs, and water can come into play.

Just as comfort is important in any interior space, it also needs to be a consideration in an outdoor area. Seating and tables are available in a range of styles and are made from durable materials that can stand up to any weather. To enhance the outdoor dining experience there are beautiful furnishings in wood, wicker, and metal that will last from season to season with cushions that dry out quickly and colorful fabrics that won't fade in bright sun. When integrating fabrics in an outdoor setting, I rely on the "springboard" method: If you already have a large established garden filled with your favorite plants, use that as a basis to find coordinating fabrics that echo your color scheme. If you are establishing a new garden and haven't settled on a color scheme, choose a neutral palette that will support your plant experiments. Some people love to change things up from year to year, so neutral fabrics give them that leeway.

Nothing has to be high maintenance. All-weather materials eliminate the bother of lugging things in and out of storage, and even the plants in ornamental pots can be irrigated on a timer. Whether your setting is under the shelter of a porch or the twinkling lights of stars, alfresco dining is a pleasure not to be missed.

Opposite, clockwise from top left: Any spot in the garden can become a relaxing retreat to enjoy a bite to eat and read a magazine; all you need are a couple of comfortable chairs and a table to hold the refreshments. A mix of colorful gourds, pumpkins, and squash casually strewn down the middle of the table makes for an easy autumn display, and as the sun sets, the votives give the centerpiece a subtle glow. Here's a breakfast nook that rivals the beauty of any interior space; fresh spring flowers adorn the table with the blooming spring garden in the background. I like no-fuss arrangements that just take minutes to put together, like this sunflower bouquet; cutting the flower stems to about 8 inches and inserting them into a presoaked piece of floral foam in a low container makes the perfect summertime centerpiece.

54. Grow a Floral Shop

Over the years I have made a deliberate attempt to fill my garden with a collection of plants that have multiple uses both inside and out. It has become almost second nature whenever I assess the value of a plant. We have so many wonderful choices that there is little need to settle for something that is merely one-dimensional. So how do you go about assessing your garden's plants for this double-duty function? Simply take a quick inventory of what you are currently growing and consider how to apply these plants to the ideas in this book or adaptations of your own. It will quickly become clear what you would like to modify or add in the future to your collection.

Here are some guidelines to consider. When I design a garden, I start with some basic "workhorse" plants. These provide the structure and serve as the background canvas for colorful flowers. Evergreens such as boxwood, yew, elaeagnus, holly, and camellias are what I use in my Zone 7 garden. From there, select some interesting deciduous shrubs that are reliable and require little maintenance. Many of the varieties I have are commonplace, such as spirea, Virginia sweetspire, quince (*Chaenomeles*), pomegranate, and roses, but they are dependable plants that are useful in many of my arrangements because of their color and bloom. Around these shrubs, fill in with perennials and bulbs that will come back year after year. In the remaining pockets, add color and bold foliage with tropical plants and annuals.

The result of this design is that you will have a garden that requires little planting each year, just the pockets of annuals and tropicals here and there, which translates to less time and money. And when you select a color scheme of plantings that complement both the exterior and interior of your home, you'll have your own private florist shop to use in an endless variety of displays.

keep sequence in mind

When choosing plants for your garden to use inside, consider varieties that will keep you in blooms and colorful foliage from early spring to the last frost. My goal, particularly when it comes to flowers, is to grow the most for the longest time. So when I select daffodils or tulips, I choose equal numbers of early, middle, and late bloomers. This extends the season from what might otherwise be a week or 10 days to more than a month. The same holds for that most glorious of all perennials, the peony. I carry this into the realm of seed as well. I plant successive rows of zinnias, celosia, and globe amaranth every 3 weeks throughout the summer for a plenitude of fresh blooms until the first hard frost.

Opposite: Planting in abundance is a key element for having enough flowers and foliage to enjoy indoors. When there are plenty of blooms, such as these large-cupped white 'Maureen' tulips, I don't hesitate to cut armloads of blossoms to bring inside or share with friends. Growing plants in large drifts also gives your garden a more spontaneous and natural appeal, since plants in the wild usually grow in large colonies.

55. Mix Produce with Flowers

As you gather items to accent your outdoor settings, rely on the beautiful qualities of fruit, flowers, and the foliage of herbs to create winning combinations. Various types of fruit from the farmers' market or grocery store make clever containers for flowers and herbs. There are so many possibilities and combinations—just let your imagination run free. For best results use fruit that has a tough skin and firm flesh. But don't let that be a limiting factor. I particularly like working with eggplant, both the dark purple type and the white. The skin is easily punctured with an ice pick or toothpick so small blooms with shorter stems can be pushed in, making the eggplant a type of "pincushion" for the flowers. However, if you plan on using the fruit as a vessel, it's important that it is easily cored out to make room for a bundle of stems. Also, once you have the fruit containers made, you can save them in the fridge, but don't forget to apply lemon juice on the cut surfaces and cover with plastic wrap to keep the flesh from discoloring. Late summer offers a bevy of fresh produce, so have some fun with it. Along with flowers, add sprigs of fragrant herbs and use patterned leaves as surfaces to display your arrangements.

Above: Granny Smith apples make a delectable little container for mini bouquets of 'Queen Sophia' and 'Tiger Eye' marigolds. The flowers are accented with sprigs of rosemary and a few leaves of golden sage. Use them as a personal arrangement for each plate or give them more impact by placing several on a striped 'Tropicana' canna leaf. **Opposite:** This delightfully simple arrangement is made by cutting the top third off a watermelon and hollowing it out. A sliver of the rind is removed from the bottom of the melon to give it a flat base. Then a piece of presoaked floral foam cut to fit in the opening is inserted to hold a bloom-to-bloom display of green 'Envy' and pink 'Enchantress' zinnias. Zinnias are such happy, easy-to-grow annual flowers. A packet of seeds will produce buckets of blooms in a rainbow of hues, so you can have flowers that are the perfect complement to your home's color palette.

VEGETABLE VESSEL

Looking for a flower holder that's fun and different? Try using an acorn squash. With just a few flowers, you can create beautiful, richly hued arrangements that are sure to be noticed in their vegetable vessel.

Colorful flowers and herbs, including zinnias, gomphrenas, scabiosa or pincushion flowers, and angelonia

Rubber band
1 squash or gourd

1. Gather a small handful of colorful flowers and herbs, and trim the stems to about 4 inches.

2. Wrap the stems with a rubber band.

3. Cut off the top quarter of the squash, scoop out the center, add a small amount of water, and drop the flowers inside.

Done!

56. Redefine Light

While we may often think of plants as giving a garden its definition, I find it is more accurate to say that light holds its complete identity. Without light there is no color, no line, no shape, no form. Darkness swallows a garden whole, enfolding it in its shadowy depths where it lies in wait to be reborn again in morning's first light. No day in the garden is the same, because each day the light changes. The sun is higher or lower in the sky, a skiff of clouds passes by, or the light is obliterated by heavy precipitation. It is only after several years and many seasons of seeing my garden in all these lights that I can say I have come to really know it.

FLOWER ARRANGER'S SECRET

If you have a wide-mouthed container and want to arrange plants with slender stems, chicken wire can help. Available in home centers, chicken wire is flexible and has a mesh pattern that can be molded into the opening of a container to provide support to stems.

Above right: Several small glass vases hold individual blooms of 'Perestroyka' tulips. **Opposite:** Bundles of daffodils seem to radiate their own light when displayed in lanterns. To make quick work of each bouquet, gather a group of flowers in one hand and cut all the stems the same length. Gently wrap a rubber band around the stems, and then place them in water-filled glass containers.

Because of my interest in garden history, I like to imagine how important lanterns and early forms of lighting must have been to gardens. Their power to bring illumination to the darkened forms in a garden must have been magical. My interest in lanterns has led me to collect as many different ones as I can. With modern lighting, I do not need to use these lanterns to illuminate my garden. Since I still want to employ my collection as decorative accents in the garden, I've found another use for them.

Using lanterns as vases to hold bouquets of flowers can be a fun twist on their intended purpose. Flame-colored tulips or bright sun-drenched daffodils can radiate their own light from the lanterns and also protect the flowers from the wind when dining outside. Often when I find used lanterns the glass is broken, but I've found that replacing it is easy and inexpensive. If the panes are simply cracked, I will not bother with patching them and let the cracks play into the charm of the object. When safety is a concern, replace the panes with Plexiglas or a clear acrylic equivalent.

Lighting in our homes and gardens brings a magical quality to an evening or a special occasion. Over the years, I've found lanterns to be an ideal way to usher in a spark of enchantment whether it is when dining alfresco or creating the effect of a garden party or picnic indoors.

One of my favorite lanterns is actually not a lantern at all but an old wire basket, reinforced with chicken wire such that it can hold nine votives. I hang it by its handle at the top of the entry arbors when I have guests. It provides just enough light to guide them into the garden after twilight and at the same time says welcome with its warm glow.

Others lanterns are less improvised and are designed to withstand gusts of wind and rain. These I place on tables, stack along the steps as a guide to guests, or hang from iron shepherds hooks in the garden. They hold votives or pillar candles, as well as battery-operated LED lights when an open flame is not possible or desired.

I've found these lanterns in the most surprising places. Some were passed down through the family, so that's what first sparked my interest in collecting them. I added more by checking out yard sales, junk shops, and flea markets. But recently, I've found great-looking lanterns in garden centers and department stores that sell interior accents and have houseware departments. They are fun to mix and match.

57. Gather a Meadow

There is something about wildflowers that captures our imagination. I suppose they represent this idea of carefree splendor, a natural gift. Whatever the reason, they have an appealing quality to novice and expert gardeners alike. Their beauty is as ephemeral as it is sublime. They must be appreciated in the moment they are in bloom. If you have access to an area where you can cut them and carry them home in a bouquet, remember that some of the same principles of cutting flowers from the garden apply here as well. Cut the flowers early in the morning using sharp shears and trim the stems on an angle to maximize the surface area for them to take up water. Place the flowers immediately into a bucket of water as you cut them. Keep the cut flowers in a cool dark place until you are ready to arrange them. Fill the vase with water and add a few drops of bleach to discourage bacteria growth and then remove any foliage from the flower stems that will be below the waterline. To lengthen the time the flowers stay fresh, display the bouquet out of direct sun in a cool area.

Growing wildflowers can be fun as well, and you don't have to live on the Ponderosa Ranch to have them close at hand. In the fall I sow the seeds in a narrow bed between my picket fence and the sidewalk with a blend designed to grow best in this area. If you'd like to give it a try there are a few tips to keep in mind. Sow the seeds in late summer and early fall so they have enough time to germinate and establish themselves before the first hard frost, usually about 8 weeks. Choose a seed blend designed for your area of the country and prepare the bed by tilling the soil to a depth of about 3 inches. Many wildflower seeds are very tiny, so mix them in a bucket with 5 parts moistened sand to 1 part seeds. Spread the mixture over the area by hand. It is critical that the seeds have good contact with the soil after they are sown, so walk over the ground or use a lawn roller. Lightly mulch the bed and keep the area consistently moist.

Above right: Brilliant red blanket flowers (*Gaillardia aristata*) carpet the field in blossoms. If you'd like to create your own meadow as a substitute to a mowed lawn, consider planting a blend of wildflowers. Native flowers are hardy and robust plants that require little care. The key is selecting a blend that is formulated to grow in your area.
Opposite: A carefree bundle of wildflowers is the perfect accompaniment to any outdoor dining table. The bouquet includes coneflowers, black-eyed Susans, coreopsis, larkspur, bachelor buttons, blanket flowers, and Queen Anne's lace. While not as long-lasting in the vase as some cut flowers, they add charm and color to any meal.

58. Create Comfortable Settings

The essence of a garden home is devoted to softening the boundaries between its interior life and the natural environment outside. Areas such as the loggia, veranda, deck, terrace, porch, or patio are located adjacent to the house and serve as junctures between these two realms. Here, flowers and foliage literally overlap with the man-made architecture and decorations of the house, becoming inseparable. Outdoor dining areas appointed with furnishings that have the look and feel of your interior decor create a vital link between house and garden. Furnishings that are similar in style and material as those you use inside help to create a seamless transition between indoors and out.

Today, decorating an outdoor setting need not be a cliché of white plastic chairs. A handsome selection of furniture and fabrics designed to withstand the elements make furnishing these areas as stylish as the rooms inside your home. Plump pillows, colorful tablecloths, and rugs infuse the area with comfort and invite guests to relax and stay awhile. And if you're not ready to invest in outdoor furnishings, consider creating a temporary setting with interior pieces. I've been known to take upholstered chairs, silver, candlesticks, and stemware and set them up in the middle of the garden. It comes as a delightful surprise to guests when they see a candlelit setting amid the flower beds.

Right: Indoor-outdoor rooms like this screened porch serve as multi-purpose areas once the weather turns warm. Comfortable furnishings give the room its cozy, welcoming feel. Whether the activity is catching a nap, enjoying a sandwich, or reading a book, there are stylish and beautiful rugs, chairs, and tables designed to withstand the elements and maintain their good looks.

59. *Make Mini-Bouquets*

When you set a table outdoors, there are very real limitations to consider. As I once found out the hard way, cut flowers don't hold up well in the hot sun, so if your event is in full sun, beware! Then, of course, there is the wind. One big gust can easily knock down a tall bouquet. Rather than cut flowers, planting garden pots of blooming flowers may be a better option.

Another solution I've found is to keep cut-flower arrangements small, well anchored, and not top heavy. Pint-sized bouquets gathered straight from the garden and dropped into small vases keep a low profile and give the table just the right splash of color. I like to collect them in the early morning, arranging them as I go into tiny nosegay-like bouquets. It's a snap to harvest a bucketful, strip the leaves, cut the stems evenly across, and wrap the bundle of stems with a rubber band. Presto! You have a tiny arrangement. Placed together, they put on quite a show.

EASY DOES IT

Avoid dropping flower frogs or pebbles into the bottom of a vase. You may not notice the vase has developed a hairline crack until it starts leaking hours later.

Top right: Zinnias are easy to grow and have a long vase life. **Bottom right:** Juice glasses are the perfect size to hold small bouquets. **Opposite:** A fast and easy way to create mini-bouquets is to arrange flowers in your hand, add single buds until you get the composition just right, and then cut the stems to the same length.

1.

2.

3.

4.

5.

6.

7.

8.

9.

PLANT COLLECTIONS

From Seed to Flower

It can be daunting to start a new garden. It's hard to suppress the desire to quickly fill the beds with blooms knowing that it takes both time and money to grow big, beautiful plants. One easy solution is to fill the borders with quick-growing annuals. While the shrubs and perennials are given time to develop, these plants balloon into colorful displays in just a few weeks. The added bonus is they make wonderful cut flowers to bring into the house. There are countless varieties in all shapes, colors, and sizes. They grow easily from seed, so you can harvest armloads of flowers for little investment.

1. 'Century Rose' celosia

2. 'Pink Gem' zinnia

3. 'Miriam' sunflower

4. 'All Around Purple' globe amaranth

5. 'Dwarf Red Plains' and 'Radiata' coreopsis

6. 'Alaska' nasturtium

7. 'Pacific Beauty' pot marigold

8. 'Messenger Rose' larkspur

9. 'Cramer's Burgundy' celosia

60. Feature Fabrics with Flowers

Never underestimate the value of outdoor fabrics to add a dramatic splash of color. Paired with the flowers and foliage in the garden, they deliver an extra punch of pattern that is awesome and easy. Inside our homes it is easy to recognize the added dimension that fabrics provide in the way of draperies, upholstery, and rugs, but we often forget their transforming effect in outdoor settings. Think of fabrics as personality you can buy by the yard. Use them to set a mood or influence the style of your outdoor areas.

TRY THE NEW PERFORMANCE FABRICS

Outdoor fabrics are designed to take whatever Mother Nature dishes out and still look beautiful. They are available in an exciting array of colors and styles and make beautiful tablecloths, napkins, pillows, curtains, and fabric-covered screens for alfresco settings.

When shopping for selections, look for fabrics that have been especially manufactured to withstand the elements. You'll find the most durable materials are those made from acrylic, solution-dyed fibers in which each strand is saturated with color (versus yarn-dyed, where just the surface is coated). Outfit outdoor settings with cushions and pillows as well as table-cloths, napkins, slipcovers for chairs, folding screens, table umbrellas, and large ground cloths for picnics. You'll be amazed at what a little fabric can do to your outdoor setting.

Above: Soft pillows in blue, green, and white make sitting in the garden even more of a delight. Not only are the colors cool and inviting, but they help enliven the outdoor display. **Opposite:** A cool spring night is warmed by the flames of a fire and by a medley of 'Perestroyka', 'Temple of Beauty', and orange parrot tulips that fill the overhead chandelier and vases on the table.

61. Create Color Blends

For many people, the thought of choosing a color scheme for their garden is almost as daunting as selecting a party menu for twenty guests. The thought is overwhelming, so to allay their fears I often counsel my clients to start with a single color and then build from there. Some are entranced with the idea of staying with their favorite color and creating a monochromatic design. The idea behind this color theme is to choose a single hue and then combine plants with variations of that color. For instance, if you choose blue, to have a monochromatic color design you would choose flowers that range from light pastel blues to shades of navy blues and intense dark blues.

Holding fast to a single color as you put together a floral arrangement can also have its advantages. The result is a simple, bold, and harmonious style that is elegant and sophisticated. However, as my clients discover when they plant a large group of flowers in the garden, those slight variations of shades among a single color is what really enlivens the look. Even the slightest difference, just one shade on either side of a single color, brings a subtle yet dynamic quality to the composition. In arrangements for outdoor settings, I find the interplay of closely related colors is similar to the dance of light and shadows over a bed of flowers. It creates a sense of movement that isn't apparent with a single-color composition. Give it a try and see if you don't think the results are more engaging and alive.

ADD ROMANCE TO OUTDOOR DINING

Find an interesting-shaped branch and wrap it with holiday lights. Hang it over an outdoor table in an open-air setting to make a unique chandelier.

Right: Tantalizing tones of yellow and orange in the lilies, columbine, kniphofia, asclepias, and santolina are on display. **Opposite:** Intriguing shades of blue, mauve, and cream hydrangeas create the appearance of light and shadows dancing over the bouquet.

62. Mix Seasons Together

Sometimes the pairing of two of our seasonal favorites
can make for a hot romance. I can't think of a better one
than the juxtaposition of fiery-colored tulips and
autumn foliage. Granted, this is an exercise in bending
a few botanical rules. Normally, tulips and fall foliage
don't appear at the same time in the garden. This is
only possible through modern technology and speedy
delivery. Some clever Dutch growers have facilities that
allow them to plant the tulip bulbs in containers, place
them in freezers for the required cooling time, and then
bring them out into greenhouses timed to be harvested
and shipped in the fall and winter. Normally, I like to
keep plants in my arrangements within the same
season, but on special occasions it's fun to mix things
up, particularly when the arrangement is part of an
outdoor setting so the contrast is even more apparent.

JUST FRESH WATER
FOR TULIPS

*While other cut flowers benefit from
floral preservatives, when it comes to
tulips, just add water. Keep the vase
clean, recut the stem ends every day or
two, and replenish the water.*

nature's color themes

Let nature's seasonal colors help you choose a palette for
your garden-home–style decor. For a spring-inspired theme,
consider the hues of new leaves, the deep purples of crocus,
and the clear bright yellows of tulips and daffodils. Shades of
summer could include the off-white colors of the snowball
bush, romantic tints of old-fashioned roses, or the pinks and
whites of fragrant honeysuckle. If fall is your favorite season,
try the fiery reds and yellows of the changing trees, bur-
nished golds and oranges of chrysanthemums and goldenrod,
and the tawny tones of the ripened grasses. Capture winter's
subtle beauty in brilliant blue skies, crisp white snow, and
black silhouettes of trees.

Whatever colors you decide on, be sure to make use of the
neutral colors of the earth and nature. The browns and
beiges of trees and the grays of stone all have a place in
garden-style decorating. And don't forget green. From the
brightest spring greens to the grayest green sage, this is the
color most associated with gardens. You can't go wrong by
using this color.

Above: Decorate glass votives by wrapping them with colorful fall leaves and securing them with a bow of natural raffia. Be sure to keep
the raffia and leaves away from the flame of the candle. **Opposite:** Tulips can be purchased any time of the year. Orange blooms blend in
beautifully with fall leaves, berried branches, and feathery plumes of ornamental grasses.

63. Clean Out Your Closets

One beautiful spring day a friend invited me to her cabin in the woods for a visit. When I arrived I could see that she had been busy washing some of her little-used dishes that had been packed away in boxes. There were stacks of dishes and various knickknacks assembled on a table that she was about to put away. I was taken by the look of her pottery and bird ornaments. On the spur of the moment, we decided to use them and created a bird-themed table setting for brunch.

KEEPING BUGS AT BAY

While the idea of a romantic outdoor dinner is wonderful, pesky insects can quickly spoil the mood. Keep bugs away with a circulating overhead fan, citronella candles, eco-friendly bug repellent, and strategically placed plants known for their insect-deterring qualities, such as citrus-scented geraniums, catmint, and marigolds.

Top right: Mixing simple plants with collectibles such as bird napkin holders and nesting bowls adds to the pleasure of the moment. **Above right:** A treasure trove of plates, containers, and trinkets is ready to be transformed into a memorable table setting. **Opposite:** Three cast-iron urns filled with seedlings of Jewels of Opar (*Talinum* 'Kingswood Gold') and a shallow iron container planted with strawberry begonias add a charming presence to this fresh-air dining table.

The nature-inspired results were delightful. Now I'm the first to admit that I'm a dyed-in-the-wool pack rat, but I'm the kind of rat that does less packing and more displaying. Granted, not everything can be pulled out and displayed, but why have this stuff if you can't see it once in a while and use it? Every year when I do spring cleaning, I'm inspired by this memory and try to challenge myself to see new ways to bring various collections together to use in fresh ways.

Floral Tools and Accessories

Floral frogs
Chicken wire
Floral snips
Pruners (for working with woody stems)
Scissors
Sharp knife
Wet foam bricks (for fresh flowers)
Wet foam cones
Mixing spoon
Dry floral foam (for dry or artificial flowers)
Waterproof florist tape
Fine florist tape (for wrapping stems)
Waterproof floral clay or gum
Floral stakes/picks/pins
Floral wire in premeasured lengths

Floral wire on reel (from 30 to 90 gauges)
U pins
Brown paper or newspaper (for conditioning tulips)
Floral preservative
Rubber bands
Stem stripper
Plastic liners/dishes or cellophane to protect vases, urns, etc.
Glue or hot glue
Sheet moss
Lazy Susan (for working on arrangements)
Decorative stones
Aquarium gravel
Screwdriver and screws
Garden twine/string

Protective cork mats
Vases, urns, dishes, bowls
Plant stand

On-line Surces and Floral Craft Supplies

www.afloral.com
www.craftsetc.com
www.hobbylobby.com
www.michaels.com
www.rolandsofcalifornia.com
www.saveoncrafts.com

Plants for Terrariums

PLANTS FOR OPEN TERRARIUMS

African violet (*Saintpaulia* spp.)
Airplant (*Kalanchoe pinnata*)
Asparagus fern (*Asparagus plumosus*)
Bird's Nest sansevieria (*Sansevieria trifasciata* 'Golden hahnii')
Bunny Ears cactus (*Opuntia microdasys*)
Earth Stars (*Cryptanthus* spp.)
Flame violet (*Episcia* spp.)
Moss sandwort (*Arenaria verna*)
Piggy-back plant (*Tolmiea menziesii*)
Rosary vine (*Ceropegia woodii*)

PLANTS FOR CLOSED OR OPEN TERRARIUMS

Airplane plant (*Chlorophytum comosum*)
Aluminum plant (*Pilea cadierei*)
Arrowhead plant (*Syngonium podophyllum*)
Artillery plant (*Pilea microphylla*)
Baby tears (*Helxine soleirolii*)
Begonias (*Begonia* spp.)
Bloodleaf (*Iresine herbstii*)
Chinese evergreen (*Aglaonema* spp.)
Creeping fig (*Ficus pumila repens*)
Croton (*Codiaeum variegatum*)
Delta maidenhair fern (*Adiantum raddianum*)
Devil's ivy (*Epipremnum aureum*)
Dwarf golden sweet flag (*Acorus gramineus minimus aureus*)
Emerald Ripple peperomia (*Peperomia caperata*)
Flame violet (*Episcia cupreata*)
English ivy (*Hedera helix*)
Foam flower (*Tiarella cordifolia*)
Gold dust dracaena *Dracaena surculosa*)
Pink polka dot plant (*Hypoestes panguinolenta*)

Heart-leaved philodendron (*Philodendron scandens oxycardium*)
Maidenhair fern (*Adiantum*)
Miniature peperomia (*Pilea depressa*)
'Moon Valley' pilea (*Pilea* spp.)
Nerve plant (*Fittonia* spp.)
Oxalis (*Oxalis* spp.)
Joseph's coat (*Alternanthera* spp.)
Prayer plant (*Maranta* spp.)
Ribbon plant (*Dracaena sanderiana*)
Satin pellionia (*Pellionia pulchra*)
Spider aralia (*Dizygotheca elegantissima*)
Strawberry begonia (*Saxifraga sarmentosa*)
Swedish ivy (*Plectranthus australis*)
Table fern (*Pteris cretica*)
Variegated oval leaf peperomia (*Peperomia obtusifolia variegata*)
Waffle plant (*Hemigraphis* 'Exotica')
Watermelon peperomia (*Peperomia sandersii*)

PLANTS FOR CLOSED TERRARIUMS

Club moss (*Lycopodium*)
Sundew (*Drosera* spp.)
Venus fly trap (*Dionaea muscipula*)

PLANTS FOR DISH GARDENS (DRY, BRIGHT LIGHT)

Echeveria (*Echeveria* spp.)
Haworthia (*Haworthia* spp.)
Hens and chicks (*Sempervivum* spp.)
Jade plant (*Crassula argentea*)
Panda plant (*Kalanchoe tomentosa*)
Stonecrop (*Sedum* spp.)

A Rose for Every Garden

CAREFREE ROSES		
'Belinda's Dream'	Large, free-flowering roses are produced on an upright shrub throughout the growing season. All the beauty of a hybrid tea with none of the worry.	Shrub, 1992, 3–6 feet, Zones 5–9, fragrant, pink blooms
'Marie Pavie'	Very versatile variety that blooms continuously throughout the season. Sweet fragrance and nearly thornless canes make it one of my favorites to enjoy indoors as a cut flower. Another perk is that it is shade tolerant.	Polyantha, 1888, 3–4 feet, Zones 5–9, fragrant, white blooms
'New Dawn'	This rose is the most carefree rose that I grow. Pale pink blooms appear all summer.	Climber, 1930, 12–20 feet, Zones 5–9, fragrant, pale pink blooms maturing to cream
'Old Blush'	I grow this beauty along my picket fence next to a burgundy barberry and purple iris. It is a heavy bloomer that requires little attention. In the fall it produces a nice display of rose hips.	China, 1752, 5–8 feet, Zones 6–9, fragrant, medium pink blooms.

ROSES THAT TOLERATE LIGHT SHADE		
'Buff Beauty'	I love apricot roses and this is one of the best. The medium-sized blooms borne in clusters perfume the air on warm days.	Hybrid musk, 1939, 5–7 feet, Zones 6–9, fragrant, apricot blooms
'Gruss an Aachen'	A favorite for lightly shaded areas. The large blooms appear repeatedly over the summer.	Floribunda, 1909, 3–4 feet, Zones 6–9, fragrant, pink blooms with hints of yellow
'Lamarque'	I have trained this rose over the door to my chicken house. It receives morning sun, but is shaded in the afternoon, yet it blooms profusely sometimes well into December.	Noisette, 1830, 12–20 feet, Zones 7–9, fragrant, pale cream blooms
'Mme. Alfred Carriere'	This rose is a vigorous climber with showy, super-fragrant blooms. In my garden it grows up through a holly hedge into the limbs of a 'Byers White' crape myrtle.	Noisette, 1879, 15–20 feet, Zones 6–9, fragrant, pale pink blooms maturing to white.

ROSES FOR COLD CLIMATES		
'Alchymist'	In spring this rose covers itself with gorgeous apricot gold flowers. It only blooms once, but the size and profusion of the blooms and its carefree nature make it a rose worth growing.	Shrub, 1956, 10–12 feet, Zones 4–9, fragrant, once-blooming, apricot blooms
'Carefree Wonder'	Large 4-inch blooms grace a compact shrub all season long. Very adaptable to a variety of growing conditions. Large orange hips in the fall.	Shrub, 1990, 3–4 feet, Zones 4–9, medium pink blooms with a white eye
'Fantin-Latour'	Although the blooms suggest the classic cabbage rose, the origins of this rose is a mystery. Flat, multipetaled pink blooms appear amid dark green foliage. The canes are nearly thornless, making this a favorite cut flower.	Centifolia (cabbage rose), unknown date of origin, 4–6 feet, Zones 4–9, fragrant, once-blooming, light pink blooms.
'Madame Plantier'	This attractive rose is planted at the corner of my front porch by the steps. Covered in clusters of white, fragrant blooms, it offers a spring greeting for guests to my home.	Alba, 1835, 4–6 feet, Zones 4–9, fragrant, once-blooming, white blooms
'The Fairy'	A great rose to plant among your favorite annuals and perennials for a lovely mixed flower border. It produces clusters of petite pink blooms all summer long. An excellent choice for small space gardens and containers.	Polyantha, 1932, 3–4 feet, Zones 4–9, light pink blooms

'Caldwell Pink'	This rose will reward you with nonstop pink flowers on a compact shrub. It requires little maintenance and will thrive in just about any soil.	Found, unknown date of origin, 3–4 feet, Zones 6–9, medium pink bloom
'Cecile Brunner'	This is a rose that has never let me down. It produces a treasure box of miniature hybrid tea-shaped blooms all summer long. I never have to spray it for black spot or insects, and it thrives in partial shade.	Polyantha, 1881, 3–4 feet, Zones 5–9, fragrant, light pink blooms
'Clotilde Soupert'	A rose that produces miniature cabbagelike blooms that are a pale cream. I find it to be a nice addition to the flower border and for containers. The fragrance is good and the plant itself it fairly carefree.	Polyantha, 1890, 3–4 feet, Zones 6–9, fragrant, white blooms
'White Pet'	As the name implies, this is a darling of a rose. Fully double, white roses adorn this diminutive shrub. It is perfect for containers or other tight spaces where you want to add blooms and fragrance	Polyantha, 1879, 2–3 feet, Zones 5–9, fragrant, white blooms

Foliage from Houseplants to Harvest and Display

Astelia chathamica 'Silver Spear'
Australian sword fern or Kimberly Queen fern (*Nephrolepis obliterate*)
Bears breeches (*Acanthus mollis*)
Bird of paradise (*Strelitzia reginae*)
Cast-iron plant (*Aspidistra elatior*)
Chinese fan palm (*Livistonia chinensis*)
Corn plant (*Dracaena fragrans* 'Massangeana')
Croton (*Codiaeum variegatum pictum*)
Dumb cane (*Dieffenbachia maculate*)

Fan plant (*Chamaerops humilis*)
Florida coontie (*Zamia floridana/pumila*)
Flowering maple (*Abutilon hybridum*)
Foxtail fern (*Asparagus meyerii*)
Ivy (*Hedera helix*)
Lady palm (*Rhapis excelsa*)
Mexican fan palm (*Washingtonia robusta*)
Mother-in-law's tongue (*Sansevieria trifasciata*)
Parlor palm (*Chamaedorea elegans*)
Prayer plant (*Maranta leuconeura*)

Pygmy date palm (*Phoenix roebelenii*)
Ribbon plant (*Dracaena sanderiana*)
Rubber plant (*Ficus elastica* 'Robusta')
Sprengeri's asparagus fern (*Asparagus densiflorus* 'Sprengeri')
Swiss cheese plant (*Monstera deliciosa*)
Tree philodendron (*Philodendron bipinnatifidum*)
Ti plant (*Cordyline terminalis*)
Umbrella plant (*Cyperus* spp.)
White bird of paradise (*Strelitzia nicolai*)

Flowering Houseplants

Adenium (*Adenium* hybrids)
African violet (*Saintpaulia* spp.)
Amaryllis (*Hippeastrum* X *acramannii*)
Cape primrose (*Streptocarpus* X *hybridus*)
Christmas cactus (*Schlumbergera* X *buckleyi*)
Crown of thorns (*Euphorbia milii* var. *splendens*)

Cylamens (*Cyclamen persicum* hybrids)
Cymbidium hybrids—orchids
Flame violet (*Episcia cupreata*)
Flaming Katy (*Kalanchoe blossfeldiana*)
Flamingo flower (*Anthurium* hybrids)
Gardenia (*Gardenia augusta*)

Moth orchids (*Phalaenopsis* hybrids)
Nun's orchid (*Phaius*)
Peace lily (*Spathiphyllum*)
Tropical lady slipper orchid (*Paphiopedilum*)
Wax plant (*Hoya lanceolata*)

Ferns that Grow Well Indoors

Asparagus fern (*Asparagus setaceus*)	Although this isn't a true fern, its feathery foliage makes it a good candidate when you want the fern look indoors. This plant does well it if has bright light, high humidity, and moist soil. Good for a hanging basket, as it has cascading stems and delicate needlelike leaves. Its best performance is in temperatures from 60 to 75 degrees F.
Bird's nest fern (*Asplenium nidus*)	Slow-growing native of tropical rain forests that is vase-shaped with shiny, light green, broad, arching leaves with ruffled edges emerging from a rosette. Size is usually 18 inches to 2 feet. It tolerates moderate indoor conditions well with a preference for temperatures between 55 and 75 degrees F, consistently moist soil, and medium humidity, though it tolerates drier air.
Boston fern (*Nephrolepis exaltata*)	Boston ferns generally aren't considered good indoor candidates because they rebel against household conditions by dropping dry foliage and making a mess. 'Dallas' or 'Dallas Jewel' is a newer compact variety that reportedly does not shed leaflets when brought indoors into lower-light conditions. Though it prefers bright indirect light and well-drained soil, it was bred to tolerate less moisture and light than most Boston ferns. Care should be taken not to overwater it. 'Fluffy Ruffles' is an older vigorous cultivar that is also compact with short fronds that appear ruffled. It, too, is reputed to be tolerant of dry indoor conditions and lower light.
Button fern (*Pellaea rotundifolia*)	A table or hanging basket fern with arching fronds made of thin dark stems and small glossy green leaflets. Some have more success with button fern because it tolerates drier conditions than most ferns. By the same token, soil that stays too wet will kill it. Prefers bright light but not direct sun.
Holly fern (*Cyrtomium falcatum*)	This fern with arching, stiff fronds of shiny, leathery, dark green leaflets tolerates tough conditions indoors and out. It can withstand drafts and low to bright light, though full sun should be avoided. It prefers moist, well-drained soil and medium humidity, but it tolerates drier conditions better than most ferns.
Kangaroo paw fern (*Microsorium diversifolium*)	Kangaroo paw fern is beautiful and easy to grow with large, erect, deeply serrated fronds of glossy green foliage and a "foot," or rhizome, that wraps around the outside of the container. Tolerant of dry air and only needs low to medium light.
Rabbit's-foot fern (*Davallia trichomanoides*) and white rabbit's-foot fern (*Humata tyermannii*)	These are plants from Fiji with furry rhizomes that creep over the sides of the pot. If planted high in a container, the "feet" can creep over the side sooner. Rabbit's-foot fern has light green, carrotlike foliage with darker feet and white rabbit's-foot fern has similar darker green foliage and white feet. Fairly easy to grow indoors but too little light and too much water can be detrimental. Best growth occurs between temperatures of 60 to 85 degrees F, though they will tolerate extremes, even frost. Preference is for bright indirect light.
Staghorn fern (*Platycerium bifurcatum*)	A hardy, slow-growing Australian native with dark green, fuzzy, antler-shaped fronds which can grow in low to medium light with no direct sun. These ferns can be grown in a pot but are often mounted on a piece of wood or bark by wrapping root ball in moist sphagnum moss with twine or fishing line or can also be grown in an orchid basket. Avoid handling fronds as they have a white, felty "scurf." 'Netherlands' is the most reliable variety, as it can tolerate more watering, which is often the death of staghorn ferns.
Table fern or Brake fern (*Pteris cretica*)	These slow-growing ferns are upright table ferns rather than hanging basket plants and they also make excellent terrarium inhabitants in their smaller stages. Their care is relatively easy if they are grown with moderate to high humidity, in well-drained moist soil, and in a cool temperature of 60 to 70 degrees F. In warmer temperatures, mist or increase humidity. An attractive variegated cultivar is 'Albo-lineata'.

Recommended Dwarf Citrus Varieties

Meyer's lemon	Bears large, sweet lemons almost year-round.
Dwarf Bears seedless lime	Large fruits ripen in winter and early spring; established plants can be everbearing.
Minneola tangelo	A grapefruit and tangerine cross; fruit ripens winter through spring.
Kaffir lime	Leaves and zest are used in Thai recipes; very fragrant leaves and unusual fruit.
Owari Satsuma mandarin orange	Seedless, juicy fruit produced in winter and early spring; hardiest of all the mandarins.

Easy-Care Houseplants

Airplane plant (*Chlorophytum comosum*)
Aloe (*Aloe barbadensis*)
Arrow head vine (*Syngonium podophyllum*)
Baby bamboo (*Poganatherum panaceum*)
Baby tears (*Helxine soleirolii*)
Blushing philodendron (*Philodendron erubescens*)
Cast-iron plant (*Aspidistra elatior*)
Chinese evergreen (*Aglaonema*)
Corn plant (*Dracaena fragrans*)
Dumb cane (*Dieffenbachia amoena*)

Dragon tree (*Dracaena marginata*)
Grape ivy (*Cissus rhombifolia*)
Heart-leaf philodendrons (*Philodendron scandens*)
Jade plant (*Crassula argentea*)
Lacy-leaf philodendron (*Philodendrun bipinnatifidum*)
Lady palm (*Rhapis excelsa*)
Mother-in-law's tongue or snake plant (*Sansevieria trifasciata*)
Parlor palm (*Chamaedorea elegans*)

Peace lily (*Spathiphyllum wallisii*)
Pothos or Devil's ivy (*Epipremnum aureum*)
Prayer plant (*Maranta leuconeura*)
Ribbon plant (*Dracaena deremensis*)
Rubber plant (*Ficus elastica*)
Schefflera (*Schefflera actinophylla*)
Swiss cheese plant (*Monstera deliciosa*)
ZZ plant (*Zamioculcas zamiifolia*)

Cut Flowers from Bulbs

Daffodil (*Narcissus* spp.)	These perennial bulbs bloom reliably from early to midspring (depending on variety) year after year and come in a range of flower shapes and sizes. Many have great fragrance. They are great in the landscape, in containers, and when used as cut flowers. For best vase life, cut when buds are very full and showing color (the gooseneck stage), as they will continue to open quickly indoors. The flower usually lasts from 4 to 6 days. Only plain tepid water is needed for daffodils, as the only preservatives that extend their vase life are regulated silver compounds available to florists. The juice from stems will plug other flower stems and shorten their life, especially tulips and anemones, so condition daffodils separately in a bucket of water for 2 hours and then arrange them in fresh water with other flowers.	Zones 3–9
Lily of the Nile (*Agapanthus* spp.)	This South African genus is grown as a tender perennial with dark green straplike, arching foliage and 4–8-inch globes of flowers in blue, purple, or white held high above foliage on stiff stalks. It has a long blooming period of up to 2 months in summer and flowers in a vase will last for weeks. Harvest when several florets are open. As new florets continue to open, older spent flowers may need to be removed occasionally to keep the arrangement looking fresh. These excellent container plants flower best when roots are crowded.	Zones 8-10
Pineapple lily (*Eucomis* spp.)	Many varieties exist of this South African native with rosettes of straplike basal leaves and thick stalks 1–2½ feet tall with small starry florets on upper half and a tuft of green on top giving the appearance of a pineapple. Florets are usually pale green with purple tints. It makes a great container plant and is long lasting as a cut flower as flowers fade to interesting seed heads on the stalk, maintaining a showy presence for 3 to 4 weeks.	Zones 7-10
Snowbells or Summer snowflake (*Leucojum aestivum*)	These heirloom bulbs from the 1500s will flower dependably year after year in midspring with two to five white bell-shaped flowers tinged with green markings on stems 12 to 18 inches. These bulbs naturalize well and tolerate moisture though not boggy soil. 'Gravetye Giant' is an improved cultivar with up to nine flowers per stem and is 22 inches tall.	Zones 3–9
Tulip (*Tulipa*)	Hybrid tulips bloom in spring from fall-planted bulbs and are spectacular planted in mass in borders and in containers. In southern climates they may need a cold treatment before planting and should be discarded as annuals after flowering. Tulips are excellent cut flowers and their vase life depends on several factors, including petal thickness of different cultivars and temperatures flowers are subjected to. Blooms may last 2 weeks in the vase, but yellowing foliage should be removed before that. Cut when flowers first open, and to keep stems from flopping, condition them by wrapping bundled stems tightly in wax paper or newspaper for several hours.	Zones 3–8
Tulip (*Tulipa clusiana* 'Lady Jane')	This dainty spring-blooming flower from fall-planted bulb returns more reliably from year to year than the larger tulip hybrids. It is a small cultivar, 10–14 inches tall, with exterior rose pink petals with a white edge and a bright white interior. Flowers should be cut as they first open, and blooms will last 3–5 days.	Zones 3–9

Cut Branches to Bring Inside

American beautyberry (*Callicarpa americana*)	This shrubby native plant, whose best feature is its beautiful fuchsia berries in fall, grows 3–8 feet tall. Full sun and good moisture will promote best flowering and fruiting. Flowers occur on new wood, which means berried branches can be cut back severely. While the berries can last 2 weeks or more, the foliage will be unsightly, as it will not hydrate. One tip is to condition stems in water 2 hours, then remove from water for 2 days so the leaves can be easily be removed, and then return the stems to water. Some florists also advise initially conditioning stems in hot water for the best vase life.	Zones 6–11
Azaleas and rhododendrons (*Rhododendron* spp.)	Hybrid evergreen azaleas and rhododendrons cultivars number in the thousands and bloom early to late spring with blooms in a wide range of colors. Flowers are numerous and showy for about 2 weeks. Hardiness varies, with many cultivars being only hardy in the South. Though not a common cut flower, branches of rhododendrons and azaleas can be cut in late winter or early spring and forced to bloom early, or stems can be cut during bloom time when half of the flowers in a cluster are open. Our blooming stems harvested in the latter way lasted in plain water about 5 to 6 days.	Zone 4–8
Bluebeard (*Caryoptera* spp.)	These small shrubs or woody perennials blooms on new wood from midsummer to fall with clusters of blue or sometimes pink flowers. In colder climates they die back to ground and return in spring. 'Sunshine Blue' has golden foliage and amethyst blue flowers that for several days in a vase. Branches from the variety 'Petit Blue' have attractive, concentrated flower clusters; it is compact and has short internodes. A new variety with pink flowers is 'Pink Chablis'.	Zones 6–8
Butterfly bush (*Buddleia davidii*)	These medium to large shrubs have large fragrant wands of flowers throughout the summer. In cold climates plants die down to ground but will resprout the next spring. Cut branches of these flowers are not long lived; flowers only last 2 to 3 days but can last 5 to 8 if conditioned by precutting underwater and putting in a floral preservative. For longer vase life, cut when only half the flowers are open. New cultivars that have large flower wands (10–12 inches) and a compact growing habit are 'Peacock' with violet flowers and 'Adonis Blue' with deep blue flowers.	Zones 5–9
Carolina moonseed (*Cocculus carolinus*)	This 10- to 14-foot adaptable vine usually grows wild in sun or shade and climbs into other trees and shrubs. It has bright red quarter-inch berries from September to December, and the berried vines can be cut and will last for weeks in arrangements.	Zones 6–9
Chinese snowball viburnum (*Viburnum macrocephalum*)	These large dense, rounded shrubs are showstoppers for several weeks in spring and early summer with profuse clusters of 1¼-inch flowers that change from green to white as they mature. Because the flowers are sterile, there are no fall berries. Plants need good drainage and in the North may need protection from cold damage. Flowering branches are spectacular in arrangements and for best vase life should be cut before flowers are completely open. Flowers can be expected to last up to 2 weeks.	Zones 6–9
Common fig (*Ficus caria*)	This coarse, broad, rounded shrub grows from 10 to 15 feet tall and has tasty fleshy fruit in summer. Common fig tree leaves are attractive, dark green, and lobed, but as far as we know their branches are not commonly used as cuts. The leaves last about 2 days in a vase without any special treatment or preservatives.	Zones 7–10
Crabapple (*Malus* spp.)	Numerous cultivars exist of this small spring flowering tree, which can offer a breathtaking spring floral display for 1 to 2 weeks and colorful fruits and foliage in fall. Cultivars should be carefully chosen, as crabapples are prone to disease and insect infestation. 'Sugar Tyme', 'Snowdrift', and 'Donald Wyman' are three recommended varieties. Flowering branches cut for the vase are usually showy for a few days up to 2 weeks. Since flowers bloom on previous year's wood, pruning should be done before June to keep from spoiling next year's flowers.	Zones 4–7
Dogwood (*Cornus florida*)	This small, native, deciduous understory tree blooms on bare branches in early spring with inconspicuous flowers surrounded by showy bracts of white or pink. Branches are often cut and forced into bloom in late winter or early spring If cutting during bloom time, harvest when bracts are beginning to open but before pollen forms. Split stems and condition in hot water and then keep in floral preservatives for a vase life of 7 to 10 days.	Zones 5–9
Eastern cottonwood (*Populus deltoides*)	This is a large tree of the eastern United States that prefers streams and bottomlands and is not typically a popular landscape tree. It's also not commonly used in floral designs, but the yellowish branches have strong angular lines and interesting, red, pendulous catkins that appear before the leaves in early spring. These last several days but are best cut when catkins are new, as they will later produce copious amounts of pollen. While the pollen from the male catkins would aggravate allergies, contrary to popular opinion, the white cottony fibers released later from the seedpods of the female trees are not allergens. (Male flowers are 3–5 inches long and have reddish stamens in a spiraling pattern; females are longer, 6–12 inches.)	Zones 3–9

Forsythia (*Forsythia* x *intermedia*)	The best feature of these large, fast-growing, deciduous shrubs with upright, arching canes is their scentless, yellow flowers that bloom very early in spring for 2 to 3 weeks. Branches can be cut in late winter and forced to bloom indoors, or stems can be cut when flowers are beginning to open. Vase life should be 1½ to 2 weeks and is enhanced with floral preservatives. 'Lynwood' is an old variety with large flowers along the entire length of the stem. New cultivars with variegated foliage and dwarf growth habit have been bred to increase the shrub's versatility.	Zones 5–8
Hydrangea, Bigleaf (*Hydrangea macrophylla*)	Popular plants that perform well with adequate moisture and partial shade by producing large colorful flowers in early summer usually on the previous year's wood, they thrive better in southern areas as severe winters can damage the bloom. Some newer varieties such as 'Endless Summer' and 'Let's Dance Starlight' also bloom on new wood to circumvent this problem. Bigleaf hydrangeas include both mopheads and lacecaps and make great cuts fresh or dried. Bloom color depends on cultivar and soil acidity where the plant is grown and ranges from white to pink, lavender, and blue.	Zones 6–9
Hydrangea, Oakleaf (*Hydrangea quercifolia*)	Improved cultivars of this native shrub have oaklike lobed leaves, good fall color, and large, beautiful, white flowers, which make beautiful fresh or dried cuts. Three of these are 'Snow Queen', 'Snow Flake', and 'Alice'.	Zones 5–9
Hydrangea, Pee gee (*Hydrangea paniculata*)	Pee gee hydrangeas are large shrubs / small trees that bloom every year on new growth in midsummer to early fall depending on the cultivar. They have white to pink conical blooms at the end of the stems and because they bloom on new growth, they will produce more flowers the following year after being cut. A vigorous variety is 'Limelight' whose large blooms are a unique chartreuse that matures to pink on strong stems with a vase life of at least 7 to 10 days. It was selected as the 2007 cut flower of the year by the Association of Specialty Cut Flowers. 'Quickfire' is a cultivar that blooms earlier than the rest and has blooms that turn dark pink.	Zones 4–8
Hydrangea, smooth (*Hydrangea arborescens*)	This low-growing, suckering shrub can be treated as an herbaceous perennial in cold climates. It produces large 6- to 12-inch white flowers on new wood in early to midsummer depending on the variety. Flowers last 1–2 months on the plants and make both excellent fresh-cut flowers and dry-cut flowers that don't shatter. 'Annabelle' and 'White Dome' are two good cultivars with large showy flowers.	Zones 3–8
Ninebark (*Physocarpus opulifolius*)	These large, hardy shrubs grow 5 to 10 feet with handsome maplelike leaves and buttonlike flowers in midsummer. Their best performance is usually in the cooler climates. Those with colorful foliage are the most desirable for landscape interest and in the vase. Some of these include 'Diablo', 'Coppertina', and a more compact cultivar 'Summer Wine'. Vase life of these branches is usually from 4 to 10 days.	Zone 3–7
Pearlbush (*Exochorda racemosa*)	The large shrub / small tree leafs out in early spring and blooms even earlier. For 1 to 2 weeks branches are covered with white scentless flowers whose unopened buds look like white pearls. These branches are showy in floral arrangements because flowers are numerous along the stems and they last about a week.	Zones 4–8
Red chokeberry (*Aronia arbutifolia*)	These large native shrubs have beautiful fall color and glossy, attractive berries in fall and winter. 'Brilliantissima' is a superior cultivar but also spreads by forming colonies like the species. The berried branches of chokeberry can be cut and used either while still green or when red. Vase life is reported to be up to 14 days.	Zones 4–9
Red maple (*Acer rubrum*)	Specimen tree grows 40–60 feet and is usually grown for its autumn foliage color. Improved cultivars should be chosen to ensure best autumn color. Spring branches make nice floral cuts owing to reddish flowers that bloom in dense clusters on bare branches followed by emerging reddish leaves that later turn green. These last about 2 weeks in water.	Zones 3–9
Shrub willow / Pussy willow (*Salix* spp.)	Grown for their attractive catkins, which appear before the leaves in early spring, these are adaptable shrubs that prefer moist soil and full sun but tolerate less. They need a period of cold to set buds so they won't do well south of Zone 7 or 8. These can also be forced in winter starting cutting in mid-February in Zones 7 and 8. Cut when brown bud stems begin to swell. 'Melanostachys' has dark stems and black catkins. *Salix chaenomeloides*, or giant pussy willow, has large catkins the size of a rabbit's foot.	Zones 4–8
Smoke tree (*Cotinus coggygria*)	Upright, multistemmed shrub or small tree that grows to 15 feet, smoke tree gets its name from the billowy hairs attached to spent flower clusters in early summer, which form pinkish clouds of color. While these make attractive cut flowers, the rounded leaves also make reliable additions to arrangements. Hybrid cultivars with purple leaves, like 'Grace', 'Royal Purple', or 'Velvet Cloak', have the most to offer as far as color in the landscape and in the vase. Cut branches last about 2 weeks. Other new cultivars with potential are 'Young Lady', a compact plant with prolific, large blooms, and 'Golden Spirit', which has foliage to match its name.	Zones 5–8

Smooth sumac (*Rhus glabra*)	This small native tree grows throughout the United States and is sometimes considered a pest, as it spreads thuggishly, replacing more desirable plants. However, it is attractive with pinnately compound leaves, astilbe-like clusters of yellow green flowers blooming in late spring or early summer, and in the fall has beautiful red foliage color and wine red cone-shaped berry clusters. Cut branches of foliage and flowers can look fresh up to a week and vase life is best if flower clusters are cut before flowers are completely open. Fall berry clusters cut while fresh look good for months. A word of caution though: while smooth sumac is not considered a poisonous plant, in some individuals who are highly susceptible to poison ivy, it can cause a rash.	Zones 3–9
Winterberry or deciduous holly (*Ilex verticillata*)	Native hollies grow in full sun to partial shade and do well in wet, poorly drained areas. The red berries on bare stems in winter are desirable for winter arrangements. A male holly should also be planted as a pollinator for the female berry-producing plants. It is recommended to cut before berries reach maturity so they will adhere to branches better and be less messy. Many cultivars exist but 'Winter Red', 'Berry Nice', and 'Berry Heavy' are good cultivars for cut arrangements, and 'Jim Dandy' is a recommended male.	Zones 3–9
Weigela (*Weigela florida*)	These shrubs with arching branches produce flowers in the spring of red, white, or pink depending on the cultivar. Varieties with variegated or burgundy foliage give added interest to the landscape and vase. 'Wine and Roses' is a cultivar with rosy pink flowers and burgundy purple foliage. Though beautiful, weigelas don't have a long vase life, usually less than a week.	Zones 5–8
Wisteria (*Wisteria* spp.)	Vigorous vine with fragrant lavender or white flower clusters in spring either before or after the foliage appears depending on the variety. For flowers that last about a week harvest when flowers first open, split the woody stems and place in warm water with floral preservative.	Zones 5–9

Air-Cleaning Plants

Areca palm (*Chrysalidocarpus lutescens*)
Australian sword fern
Boston fern (*Nephrolepis exaltata* 'Bostoniensis')
Chinese evergreen (*Aglaonema modestum*)
Cornstalk dracaena (*Dracaena fragrans* 'Massangeana')
Dwarf date palm (*Phoenix roebelenii*)
Elephant ear philodendron (*Philodendron domesticum*)

English ivy (*Hedera helix*)
Golden pothos (*Epipremnum aureus*)
Heartleaf philodendron (*Philodendron scandens* 'Oxycardium')
Janet Craig dracaena (*Dracaena deremensis* 'Janet Craig*)
Peace lily (*Spathiphyllum* 'Mauna Loa')
Red-edged draraena (*Dracaena marginata*)
Reed palm (*Chamaedorea sefritzii*)

Rubber plant (*Ficus elastica*)
Selloum philodendron (*Philodendron selloum*)
Snake plant (*Sansevieria trifasciata*)
Spider plant (*Chlorophytum comosum*)
Warneck dracaena (*Dracaena deremensis* 'Warneckii')
Weeping fig (*Ficus benjamina*)

Big-Foliage Plants

Banana leaves (*Musa*)
Bird of paradise (*Strelitzia reginae*)
Canna (*Canna* spp.)
Castor bean 'Carmencita' (*Ricinus communis*)
Cucumber magnolia (*Magnolia acuminata*)

Date palm (*Phoenix dactylifera*)
Elephant ears (*Alocasia macrorrhiza* and *Colocasia esculenta*)
Gunnera (*Gunnera manicata*)
Japanese rice paper plant (*Tetrapanax papyriferus*)

Japanese aralia (*Fatsia japonica*)
Plume poppy (*Macleaya cordata*)
'Queen Sago' palm (*Cycas circinalis*)
Rhubarb (*Rheum*)

Plant Collections: Houseplants

Airplane plant (*Chlorophytum comosum*)	This South African native has been a popular houseplant for many years because of its looks as well as being easy to grow and propagate. When displayed in hanging baskets the variegated grasslike leaves and the wiry cascading stems holding clusters of baby plants tumble over the sides of the container. High humidity isn't necessary, but plants prefer consistently moist soil, medium to bright indirect light, and temperatures between 60 and 75 degrees F.
Croton (*Codiaeum variegatum*)	This shrublike native of Malaysia, Australia, and the Pacific Islands has tough, leathery leaves and is often grown outdoors and brought in to overwinter. Though it rarely blooms in cultivation, the colorful leaves can have combinations of green, yellow, pink, and orange. Many cultivars exist with a variety of leaf shapes from long and broad, to deeply lobed, to slender and wavy. These are usually sold unnamed. Its preference is for bright light, very high humidity, consistent moisture, and moderate temperatures with a minimum of 60 degrees F at night.
Chinese jade plant (*Crassula ovata arborescens*)	This succulent has interesting fleshy leaves and a treelike form with thick stems and multiple branches. It needs bright light and can take sun in winter. Let the soil dry out between waterings and avoid getting water on the leaves of the plant. It can withstand cool conditions, especially in winter where temperatures can drop to 55 or even 45 degrees F. The plant prefers its roots to be somewhat crowded in a smaller pot and will stop growing if planted in too large a container. It can also result in a plant with thin branches and floppy leaves.
Echeveria 'Afterglow' (*Echeveria* hybrids)	Echeverias are beautiful foliage plants with short rosettes of fleshy leaves and stalks with long-lasting flowers. 'Afterglow' is a vigorous variety that is one of the prettiest with 12-inch rosettes of powdery lavender gray leaves with a bright pink edge. They are drought-tolerant plants that will take shade but have their best color in sun. They can survive temperatures as low as 20 degrees F.
Echeveria (*Echeveria nodulosa*)	This slow-growing succulent has 8- to 12-inch stems that emerge from rosettes of blue-green foliage with unusual red markings on the leaf interiors and edges. In spring it has pinkish white flowers.
'Miami Storm' begonia (*Begonia rex-cultorum*)	A rex begonia hybrid, also called a fancy-leaf begonia, is from a series called Great American Cities that are bred not to go dormant like most rex begonias do during short winter days. Plants are from 6 to 12 inches tall and are grown not for its occasional bloom but for its beautiful foliage with leaves that are metallic red with a darker starburst in the center. Rex begonias that are actively growing need bright light, high humidity, and are best in temperatures between 60 to 75 degrees F.
Oncidium orchid	Recommended for growing in the home, oncidiums are epiphytic and have pseudobulbs to store water and nutrients. They come in many colors with several flowers on each spike. After blooming it is recommended to cut the spike 2 inches below the last flower to promote additional spiking and blooming. They enjoy very bright light and do well near a window in the east or west or with filtering in a south window. Best temperatures are between 60 and 80 degrees F, and they need watering 2–4 times a week depending on temperature and light conditions. Some cultivars can tolerate less humidity than other orchid types, but to increase humidity, set plant on pebbled tray of water.
Peace lily (*Spathiphyllum wallisii*)	This South American native with large, glossy leaves and white spathelike flowers is tolerant of difficult indoor conditions. It also has the reputation of helping filter pollutants from the air. It likes high humidity, consistent watering, and temperatures between 65 and 75 degrees F. It prefers bright, filtered light (no direct sun) but will tolerate low-light conditions.
White rabbit's-foot fern (*Humata tyermannii*)	Dark green carrotlike foliage and furry rhizomes that creep over the sides of a pot characterize this fern. It is fairly easy to grow indoors, but too little light and too much water can be detrimental. Best growth occurs between temperatures of 60 and 85 degrees F, although it will tolerate extremes, even frost. Preference is for bright indirect light.

Astelia (*Astelia chathamica* 'Silver Spear')	This great specimen or container plant from New Zealand has a unique, clumping habit and silvery straplike leaves. Plant reach 4 feet tall and 6 feet wide and tolerate full sun to partial shade but cannot survive poorly drained soil. Hardiness is to 20 degrees F.	Zones 8–9
Azalea and rhododendron (*Rhododendron* spp.)	Hybrid azaleas and rhododendrons are treasured shrubs that bloom prolifically in early to late spring in a wide range of colors. Many are evergreen, extending their usefulness in the landscape. Rhododendron usually refers to the large-leaf types with large terminal flower clusters, and azalea refers to the deciduous and small-leaf evergreen hybrids with smaller clusters of funnel-shaped flowers. Encore azaleas are a new series released a few years ago that are evergreen and bloom in spring and then rebloom in summer and fall. Compact varieties of these exist that are suitable not only for the landscape but also for containers with multiseason appeal. 'Autumn Coral', 'Autumn Cheer', 'Autumn Carnival', and 'Autumn Embers' are varieties that grow to 3 feet or less.	Zones 4–8
Bigleaf hydrangea (*Hydrangea macrophylla*)	Popular plants that perform well with adequate moisture and partial shade by producing large, colorful flowers in early summer usually on the previous year's wood, they thrive better in southern areas as severe winters can damage the bloom. Some newer varieties such as 'Endless Summer' and 'Let's Dance Starlight' also bloom on new wood to circumvent this problem. Bigleaf hydrangeas include both mopheads and lacecaps and make great cuts fresh or dried. Bloom color depends on cultivar and soil acidity where the plant is grown and range from white to pink, lavender, and blue.	Zones 6–9
Bluebeard (*Caryopteris* spp.)	These small shrubs or woody perennials bloom on new wood from midsummer to fall with clusters of blue or sometimes pink flowers. In colder climates they die back to the ground and regrow in spring. 'Sunshine Blue' has golden foliage that is showy in spring and early summer before amethyst flower clusters appear. 'Petit Blue' has tight compact growth and short internodes that create an intense floral display, and 'Pink Chablis' is a variety with pink flowers.	Zones 6–8
Century plant (*Agave americana*)	This Mexican native has large, stemless rosettes of stiff gray leaves with sharp tips and teeth and is valued for its clean, sculptural outline in the garden and in containers. In cooler climates it is often grown in a container and moved to a protected area in winter. It can be enjoyed indoors as a houseplant in winter, as it tolerates dry air conditions well and only needs infrequent watering. It will need bright light from a sunny window and adequate space so that its sharp tips do not harm people and pets.	Zones 9–10
'Christmas Bells' heather (*Erica canaliculata*)	Also called black-eyed heather, this evergreen shrub with tiny green leaves is smothered December through May with numerous tiny, nearly white or pale pink urn-shaped flowers with black centers. Plants reach 3–6 feet tall and prefer mildly acidic, consistently moist soil with good drainage. They are frost tender but prefer regions with cool summers. Their winter bloom time makes them excellent candidates for indoor potted holiday plants. Their blooms and foliage are also valued as long-lasting cut flowers.	Zones 9–10
Christmas rose (*Helleborus niger* 'HGC Josef Lemper')	Hellebores are hardy perennials. Most are evergreen with dark green leathery foliage. Christmas rose is one hellebore that can bloom from December to April in mild climates. Because of this tendency it makes an excellent potted plant to bring indoors in winter. 'HGC Josef Lemper' is 8–10 inches tall and has white outward-facing, rather than nodding, flowers on sturdy stems. The flowers and plant tolerate indoor conditions if kept somewhat cool, and buds may continue to appear and bloom for 2 to 3 weeks. In spring it can then be added to a shaded perennial garden. Winter rose, or *Helleborus* x *nigercors* 'Green Corsica', is similar with compact growth, white flowers that mature to green, and a bloom time of February to March. It, too, can be enjoyed indoors in winter also.	Zones 4–8
Clematis (*Clematis* hybrids)	This deciduous flowering vine needs support for its leaves and thin stems that twine and clasp around objects as it grows. It is often planted to grow into shrubs and trees. Flowering time is usually spring and summer but it varies, because depending on variety, flowers occur on new wood, old wood, or both. Clematis often grow 10–20 feet but compact varieties exist that are suitable for growing in containers. The recommendation is that with proper fertilization and pruning, clematis can be grown in containers at least 2–3 years without any decline. Some recommended compact cultivars are 'Climador', 'Pink Climador', 'Ruutel', 'Bee's Jubilee', 'Josephine', 'Sugar Candy', and 'Mrs. N. Thompson'.	Zones 4–9
Daffodil (*Narcissus* spp.)	These perennial bulbs bloom reliably from early to midspring (depending on variety) year after year and come in a range or flower shapes and sizes. Many have great fragrance. They are great in the landscape, in containers, and when used as cut flowers. Bulbs can be planted in nursery containers in fall, subjected to a cold period, and brought out to bloom and enjoy indoors in late winter or early spring. If indoor temperatures are cool these can last a week or more. Bulbs can then be planted outdoors to recover and bloom in landscape in successive years.	Zones 3–9

Dutch hyacinth (*Hyacinthus orientalis*)	Large clusters of florets bloom on 8- to 10-inch stalks in spring from fall-planted bulbs. Flowers come in many rich colors and have intense fragrance. Bulbs will perennialize and bloom in subsequent springs, but stems will have fewer florets less densely arranged. Bulbs are good for forcing in nursery pots to bring indoors to enjoy fragrance. If purchasing forced hyacinths, look for pots where only a few florets are open to enjoy maximum blooming life of the plant, which should be approximately 1–2 weeks.	Zones 4–8
English boxwood (*Buxus sempervirens* 'Suffruticosa')	These compact, slow-growing evergreen shrubs with small, dark green leaves are ideal for edging and topiaries that will only reach 4–5 feet tall after many years and can be pruned to remain only a few inches high. Their controllable stature also makes them good candidates for containers. Boxwoods grow in both sun and shade, need protection from harsh winds and severe cold, and perform best in well-drained soils with a high pH. English boxwoods' very thick foliage makes them susceptible to fungal disease. Thinning the foliage in winter helps prevent this and also provides cuttings for winter arrangements.	Zones 5–8
Forsythia (*Forsythia* x *intermedia*)	The best feature of these large, fast-growing, deciduous shrubs with upright, arching canes is their scentless, yellow flowers that bloom very early in spring for 2 to 3 weeks. Sometimes they take on a reddish purple fall color. Potted specimens brought indoors bloom up to 2 weeks if conditions are kept cool. 'Lynwood' is an old variety with large flowers along entire length of stem. New cultivars with variegated foliage and dwarf growth habit have been bred to increase the shrub's versatility.	Zones 5–8
Grape hyacinth (*Muscari* spp.)	These small, hardy, vigorous spring bloomers are 4–8 inches tall with narrow, tubular leaves and sweetly scented clusters of bell-shaped flowers in shades of blue and white. Grape hyacinths perennialize and bloom every year from fall-planted bulbs. They are good in the landscape and forced in containers. 'Valerie Finnis' is an unusual cultivar with clear light blue, tightly formed flowers.	Zones 4-9
Japanese pieris (*Pieris japonica*)	This attractive evergreen shrub has pendulous, long-lasting clusters of bell-shaped white, pink, or dark rose blooms beginning in early spring and sometimes lasting 6–8 weeks. Prefers acidic soil and partial shade to shade. Some cultivars also have brilliant red new growth in spring and in winter burgundy foliage. 'Valley Valentine' has red buds that open to long-lasting pink flower clusters.	Zones 5–9
Lily of the Nile (*Agapanthus* spp.)	This South African genus is grown as a tender perennial with dark green straplike, arching foliage and 4–8-inch globes of flowers in blue, purple, or white held high above foliage on stiff stalks. Some varieties are hardy in Zones 6 and 7. It has a long blooming period of up to 2 months in summer, and flowers in a vase will last for weeks. These excellent container plants flowers best when roots are crowded.	Zones 8–10
Pansy (*Viola* x *wittrockiana*)	Modern hybrid pansies are cold-hardy annuals planted in spring and fall, providing masses of 2- to 3-inch blooms. In mild climates they will often bloom in winter during warm spells. Plants respond well to frequent fertilization and consistent moisture. Violas (*Viola cornuta*), similar plants with smaller, more numerous blooms are more weather tolerant. Pansies and violas also make good container plants. These can tolerate being brought indoors for a few days and will suffer less in bright light and cool temperatures.	Zones tk
Pineapple lily (*Eucomis* spp.)	Many varieties exist of this South African native with rosettes of straplike basal leaves and thick stalks 1–2½ feet tall with small starry florets on upper half and a tuft of green on top giving the appearance of a pineapple. Florets are usually pale green with purple tints. It makes a great container plant, and flower stalks remain showy for weeks as flowers fade to interesting seed heads on the stalk. 'Sparkling Burgundy' is an unusual variety with gorgeous, reddish purple foliage.	Zones 7–10
Spirea (*Spirea thunbergii* 'Ogon')	These compact, bushy, willow-leafed deciduous shrubs reach 3 feet tall and have attractive yellow green foliage after white flowers that bloom on bare, arching branches in early spring have faded. Fall foliage is bronze. Their compact size and three-season appeal make them good container plants. *Spirea fritschiana* 'Pink Parasols' is another compact variety under 3 feet tall and has large pink blooms, blue-green leaves, and orange-red autumn color.	Zones 4–8
Weigela (*Weigela florida*)	This shrub with arching branches produces flowers in the spring of red, white, or pink depending on the cultivar. Varieties with variegated or burgundy foliage give added interest to the landscape and vase. Two compact varieties with pink flowers that can be used in containers and in the front of borders are 'My Monet' with variegated foliage and 'Fine Wine' with burgundy foliage.	Zones 5–8

Flowers for Drying

Baby's breath (*Gyposphila paniculata*)
Bachelor's buttons (*Centaurea cyanus*)
Celosia (*Celosia*)
Gomphrena (*Gomphrena*)

Hydrangea (*Hydrangea* spp.)
Larkspur (*Consolida ambigua*)
Lavender (*Lavandula*)
Roses (*Rosa* spp.)

Statice (*Limonium*)
Strawflowers (*Smilacina stellata*)

Grasses, Plumes, and Leaves for Drying

Black millet (*Pennisetum glaucum*)
Broom corn (*Sorghum*)
Chinese Fan Palm (*Livistonia chinensis*)
Eucalyptus (*Eucalyptus* spp.)

Fountain grass (*Pennisetum* spp.)
Horsetail reed (*Equisetum hyemale*)
Miscanthus (*Miscanthus* spp.)
Pampas grass (*Cortaderia* spp.)

Sea oats (*Chasmanthium latifolium*)
Sweet Annie (*Artemisia annua*)

Dried Seeds and Pods

Allium (*Allium* spp.)
Artemisia (*Artemisia* spp.)
Blackberry lily seeds (*Belamcanda chinenis*)
Lotus (*Nelumbo nucifera*)

Okra (*Hibiscus esculenta*)
Money plant (*Lunaria annua*)
Nigella seed pods (*Nigella damascena*)
Poppy seedpods (*Papaver* spp.)

Setaria (*Setaria* spp.)
Sweetgum balls (*Liquidambar styraciflua*)

Fresh Seeds and Pods

American bittersweet berries (*Celastrus scandens*)
Beautyberry berries (*Callicarpa americana*)
Butterfly weed 'Oscar' seedpods (*Gomphocarpus physocarpus*)

Canna seedpods (*Canna* spp.)
Carolina moonseed berries (*Cocculus carolinus*)
Echinacea seed heads (*Echinacea* spp.)
Hyacinth bean pods (*Dolichos lablab*)

Ligustrum berries (*Ligustrum* spp.)
Rose hips (*Rosa*)
Winterberry berries (*Ilex verticillata*)

Adams, William Howard. *Jefferson's Monticello.* New York: Abbeville Press, 1983.

Beales, Peter. *Classic Roses—An Illustrated Encyclopeadia and Grower's Manual of Old Roses, Shrub Roses and Climbers.* New York: Henry Holt & Company, 1997.

Brooks, John. *The Indoor Garden Book.* New York: Crown, 1986.

Bryan, John M. *Biltmore Estate: The Most Distinguished Private Place.* New York: Rizzoli, 1994.

Chatto, Beth. *The Green Tapestry: Choosing and Grouping the Best Perennial Plants for Your Garden.* New York: Simon and Schuster, 1989.

Chefetz, Shelia. *Antiques for the Table.* New York: Penguin Books, 1993.

De Bay, Phillip, and James Bolton. *Garden Mania—The Ardent Gardener's Compendium of Design and Decoration.* London: Thames and Hudson, 2000.

De Nicolay-Mazery, Christiane. *The French Country House.* New York: The Vendome Press, 2003.

Griffiths, Sally, and Simon McBride. *The English House: English Country Houses & Interiors.* New York: Rizzoli, 2004.

Hadfield, Miles. *Topiary and Ornamental Hedges.* London: A & C Black, Limited, 1971.

Ireland, Kathryn M. *Classic Country.* Layton, Utah: Gibbs Smith, 2007.

Jekyll, Gertrude, and Lawrence Weaver. *Gardens for Small Country Houses.* London: Antique Collector's Club, 1981.

Jones, Chester. *Colefax & Fowler: The Best in English Interior Decoration.* Great Britain: Barrie & Jenkins, 1989.

Lacy, Allen. *The Gardener's Eye and Other Essays.* New York: Grove/Atlantic, 1992.

Lacy, Allen, and Christopher Baker. *The Glory of Roses.* New York: Stewart, Tabori & Chang, 1990.

Lawrence, Elizabeth. *Gardening for Love.* Durham, NC: Duke University Press, 1987.

———. *The Little Bulbs: A Tale of Two Gardens.* Durham, NC: Duke University Press, 1986.

Leighton, Ann. *Early American Gardens.* New York: Houghton Mifflin, 1970.

Lewis, Adam. *Albert Hadley.* New York: Rizzoli, 2005.

Listri, Massimo. *Where the Muses Dwell: Homes of Great Artists and Writers.* New York: Rizzoli, 1996.

Lutyens, E. L. *Houses and Gardens.* London: Antique Collector's Club, 2004.

Magnani, Denise. *The Winterthur Garden: Henry Francis du Pont's Romance with the Land.* New York: Harry N. Abrams, 2004.

Maynard, W. Barksdale. *Architecture in the United States, 1800–1850.* New Haven, CT: Yale University Press, 2002.

Miller, Mary Warren, Ronald W. Miller, and David King Gleason (photographer). *The Great Houses of Natchez.* Jackson, MS: University Press of Mississippi, 1998.

Morris, Alistair. *Antiques from the Garden.* London: Garden Art Press, 1998.

Plumptre, George. *Garden Ornament—Five Hundred Years of History and Practice.* London: Thames and Hudson, 1989.

Pryke, Paula. *Table Flowers: Innovative Floral Designs for Entertaining.* New York: Rizzoli, 2007.

Rix, Martyn E., and Roger Phillips. *The Bulb Book: A Photographic Guide to Over 800 Hardy Bulbs.* London: Pan Books, 1960.

Sherwood, Shirley. *Contemporary Botanical Artists.* New York: Sterling, 1996.

Sully, Susan. *The Southern Cottage: From the Blue Ridge Mountains to the Florida Keys.* New York: Rizzoli, 2007.

Thorpe, Patricia. *Growing Pains: Time and Change in the Garden.* New York: Harcourt Brace, 1994.

Tolpin, Jim. *A Cottage Home.* Taunton, CT: New Edition, 2000.

Tripp, Kim E., and J. C. Raulston. *The Year in Trees: Superb Woody Plants for Four Season Gardens.* Portland, OR: Timber Press, 1995.

White, Katherine. *Antique Flowers.* New York: Villard Books, 1988.

Whiteside, Katherine. *Antique Flowers: A Guide to Using Old-Fashioned Species in Contemporary Gardens.* New York: Villard Books, 1989.

Williams, Bunny, and Christine Pettel. *An Affair with a House.* New York: Stewart, Tabori and Chang, 2005.

Wood, Martin. *Nancy Lancaster: English Country House Style.* London: Frances Lincoln, 2005.

ACKNOWLEDGMENTS

My thanks to Sheb Fisher and Betty Freeze for their assistance in creating and styling the ideas you see on these pages. Also to Jane Colclasure and Kelly Quinn for capturing the spirit of the garden indoors with their artful eye and to Catherine Gilbert for coordinating the shoots and the photos. Thanks to Betsy Lyman, who transformed my stories and scribbles into text that stayed true to my voice and meaning.

A special note of gratitude to many friends who graciously opened their beautiful homes and gardens to be included in this book: Sheb and Danny Fisher, Cary and Page Wilson, Somers and Andy Collins, Becky and Reed Thompson, Susan and Rick Smith, Cheryl and Mark Nichols, Kim and Tom Booth, and Nancy and Duncan Porter.

Many at Clarkson Potter did their part to mold and shape the book into its final form, particularly publisher Lauren Shakely, editorial director Doris Cooper, and editors Amy Pierpont and Judy Pray. Jane Treuhaft and Marysarah Quinn's creative direction along with Dina Dell'Arciprete's design gave the book its style. Mark McCauslin and Joan Denman kept the book on schedule, and Kate Tyler and Selina Cicogna got the word out about the book.

For the daily support of all the other members of my staff who are instrumental to the success of Hortus, Ltd., I say thanks: Mary Ellen Pyle, David Curran, David Duncan, Pam Holden, Laura Leech, Holly Lewis, Todd Orr, Bill Rech, Bill Reishstein, Bill Ridlehoover, Suzanne Selby, Mandy Shoptaw, Brent Walker, and Elba Benitz.

My gratitude also extends to my wonderful friends, family, and clients who have been a constant support and offered their talents toward my endeavors, including Susan, Rich, Graceleigh, and Sawyer Wright; J.P., Ericka, Julian, Sophie, and Ethan Francoeur; Anthony Shoptaw; Teri and Ray Bunce; Ken and Ellen Hughes; Brian Hardin; Warren and Harriet Stephens; Sally Foley; Carl Miller, Jr.; Claiborne and Elaine Deming; Rick Smith and Susan Sims Smith; Kim and Mark Brockinton; Cheryl and Mark Nichols; Jim Dyke and Helen Porter; Cathy Hamilton Mayton and Mike Mayton; Charlotte and Robert Brown; Jim and Janice Goodwin; Reed and Becky Thompson; Kelle Mills; Gaye and Robert Anderson; Ann West; Henry and Marilyn Lile; Doug Buford; Kathy Graves; members of the Little Rock Garden Club;

Justin Slarks; Stephen Christenson; Robert and Mary Lynn Dudley; Jay and Patsy Hill; the Stella Boyle Smith Charitable Trust; John Jacoby; Kay and Overton Anderson; Bob and Marilyn Bogle; David Paul Garner, Jr., and Marlsgate Plantation; Butch and Sissi Bennett; Maynard Hannah; Jerry Phillips; Fred and Margaret Carl; Becky Clements; and Kelly Pruitt.

My gratitude also extends to the many companies that have been instrumental in their support: ABC Carpet and Home, Ag-Pro Companies–John Deere, Al Bar Wilmette, Anthropologie, Jason Garner of Antique Brick Company, B. A. Framer, Benjamin Moore, Bennett Brothers Stone Company, BioBased, Bonnie Plant Farms, Boulevard Bread Company, Brea Water, Central Garden and Pet, Circa Lighting, Classic Marble & Granite, Cynthia East Fabrics, Dawn Solar, Susan Henry of Cobblestone and Vine, Dillard's Inc., DuPont Building, DuPont Landscape, European Garden, Ferry Morse Seed Company, Follansbee, Garden Safe, Georgia Pacific, GJ Styles, GKI Lighting, Global Views, Hickory Chair, Homespice Décor, J. Poker and Sons, Jiffy Products, John Deere, Kohler, Laneventure, Lee Industries, Lennox Hearth, Lennox, Marvin Windows, Merida Meridian, Messina, Michaelian Home, Mitchell/Gold, New England Pottery, Norcal Pottery, Oly, Premier Horticultural Soil, Pro-Mix, Proven Winners including Euro American, Four Star Greenhouse, and Pleasant View Gardens, Quail Valley Grasses, Rainbird, Restoration Tile, River Road Farms, Spectrum, Stihl, Subaru, Sunbrella, Susan Henry of Cobblestone and Vine, Timberlane, Tractor Supply Company, Trio's, UpCountry Living, Vagabond, Viking Range Corporation, Walpole, Woodworkers, Wildseed Farms, and Williams-Sonoma. Thanks also to Margee Rader for providing her purse topiary design and to D. Francis White and Jerry Lee Dorrough for several paintings in my home.

To my associates on the garden design team for their hard work and talent in helping me create and maintain our clients' beautiful gardens: Ward Lile, Nicole Claas, Sarah Burr, Lorri Davis, Aaron Ruby, Wes Parson, Josh Lindsey, Josh Boykin, Antonio Cruz, Jose Sanchez, Frankie Ramirez, David Morris, and especially my brother, Chris Smith, who keeps things rolling in the right direction along with the Garden Home Retreat staff of Enrique Sanchez, Humberto Sanchez, and Antonio Garcia.